# "VISION 54"

*"The greatest golf story ever written."*

By

**Dudley Peters**

# Dedication

I have long believed that golf is the greatest game ever invented by mankind. This view is upheld by the countless friendships molded and shaped by events on the course. As such, this book is dedicated to the many friends I have met through golf.

# Table of Contents

# Chapter 1

He turned 16 years old today. His mind was wondering, as he was still lying in his bed just before sun-up; How he could go about getting and owning his own set of golf clubs.

Most every American kid, when turning 16, thought only about getting their driving license, but not him. His thoughts were about golf. He loved playing golf. Yes, he loved everything about it.

He knew that there would be no golf clubs coming to him for his birthday. Sets were expensive, and his parents could not afford to buy them.

The golf course, "Briar Lakes Golf Club," for which he already had his second summer *work permit*, was less than a mile from where he lived.

He got this summer job there from the head pro after he asked him if he could work there until school re-opened. The pro knew the boy by seeing him quite often hanging around the course with some of the other young boys whose parents were members, but his parents were not.

The job, and the main chore assigned to him, was to tidy up, check the batteries, wash and clean the electric golf carts as they came in, plus keep the range ball machine clean and loaded for the members there, it was the exact same assignment he had last year.

VISION 54<br>by Dudley Peters

Whenever he and his buddies could, they would play a few holes of golf, here and there, and sometimes, when there were almost no members playing on the course, Henry and his buddies would play all day.

During the two long summer seasons, the boys played a lot of golf there, a lot of golf, especially on Mondays, when there were practically no members scheduled.

Sometimes from daybreak 'til dark. In the summer, that was a long day, about fifteen or sixteen hours. Many times, Henry's buddies had to go home for dinner and other things, but this didn't bother Henry in the least. He never tired of hitting balls; he would hit balls until there was almost total darkness. His buddies all had their own clubs and bags, as for himself, he would use clubs that were held in the lost club bin, which was kept in the bag room at the clubhouse.

The bag he used was one that was discarded by its former owner. It was pretty much worn out, but Henry would make it do.

Many times, when the bin only had a poor selection of clubs to pick from, Henry would play a round with only 4 or 5 clubs. He didn't know it then, but this is an excellent way to get good at playing golf. Really good.

While learning to play this way, he taught himself how to adjust his grip, stance, and swing to change a club's dynamics into something other than that for which it was designed. This way, he could make the trajectory, high or low, and he taught himself how to change the <u>distance</u> of the shot, (the most important part of any golf shot.) He learned how to do whatever was called for to carry off an important golf shot. He had never taken a golf lesson. He would simply just watch some of the better players hit balls when he could. All the rest of his abilities and adjustments came to him naturally. Yes, Henry was a natural with a great sense of balance and control of his body, all necessary assets to become a competitive golfer.

During the long summer days, Henry and his buddies played golf and spent quite a lot of time hitting balls on the driving range and putting green. They figured out ways to challenge each other too. These types of challenges and games lent themselves to sharpening the abilities of the boys, some more than others. It went unnoticed by them, but all the while, they were getting better and better. Henry was much better, and his buddies all knew it.

Whenever his buddies had other things to do after work, Henry would stay back by himself and hit balls. Sometimes, he would hit the same club 200 or more times in a row so he could learn how to dominate a particular club. He also would putt the same putt over and over again. He never got tired of practicing. He loved it, and somehow he was driven.

Henry had read somewhere that Tiger Woods had hit over 6 million golf shots. This number stuck in Henry's mind. He knew that it would take quite some time to hit even 100,000 golf shots, much less 6 million. But he took it upon himself to do it any way he could. Needless to say, he would spend many, many hours on the range.

Typically, there are approximately 120 golf balls in a "large bucket." So, a player would need to hit, mathematically, 8,350 large buckets to complete 1 million golf shots. (So, if you were to hit 5 large buckets (600 balls) every day, seven days a week, it would take a bit more than 4.5 years to reach a million shots.)

*"Except for the Touring Pros, nearly <u>all</u> <u>other golfers</u> sense the feel of the <u>perfect connection, of a pure golf stroke</u>, maybe once or twice in an entire year. Some golfers never feel it, and most never will."*

There are several reasons for players hitting this many golf shots. Most of all, it is seeking, or learning, how to hit a golf ball with the much sought-after, <u>pure stroke</u>.

Another reason is *muscle memory*. Every golf shot requires the necessary movement of certain muscles and bones. The best golfers have such a memory coming from repeated natural movements brought about solely because they have done it so many times.

(When I say many times, I'm talking a million or more. Very few amateurs have ever attained that many golf strokes.)

It does not matter which type of shot a pro golfer is planning, part of this needed *muscle memory* will automatically be implemented.

VISION 54
by Dudley Peters

The Pro at Briar Lakes never complained about Henry practicing or playing, as long as he didn't neglect his work assignments. Occasionally, the pro would even point out to Henry some things, or habits to avoid when learning a good swing.

After working there, starting 3 summers now, the pro saw the natural talent the kid had. Also, he was impressed by his attitude and manners. He was appreciable, respectful, dependable, punctual, and he was honest, all necessary behaviors for a legitimate golfer. Yes, Henry was gifted, and also, he was a natural.

The pro just knew there was something different with this kid. He felt certain that one day, he would turn pro and do something great. Just what, of course, he didn't know.

Nobody did.

# Chapter 2

Henry Ulysses Muller was his name; all his friends called him "Hummer," including his family members. Hummer was born in Washington, D.C. His parents lived on the outskirts of Washington D.C., in Rockville, Maryland; his mother was a homemaker, and his father was a government employee with the Census Bureau.

Hummer had two sisters, one older and one younger than himself. Susan was the oldest at eighteen, and Joanie was the youngest; she was fifteen. Joanie and Hummer almost shared the same birthdays; she was born just three days after his first birthday.

Susan knew almost nothing about golf; she was sociable and outgoing, and she had no athletic qualities whatsoever. She was preparing to go to college at the University of Maryland in September. She wanted to become CPA. The younger sister, Joanie, however, was into athletics; she was a gymnast and a tennis player. She did fairly well at both. She was also a prankster and seemed to always be laughing and having a good time. She was happy and personable, plus she was well-liked. She proved to be extremely popular among her teenage peers, and she relished it.

Neither Hummer's parents, nor his older sister knew anything of his abilities regarding golf, but his little sister Joanie did. She often inquired about his game, and she even played with him on a couple of occasions. His golfing abilities were impressive to her. Once, she caddied for him in a non-sanctioned match play challenge, which he won.

Hummer and his buddies continued playing a lot of golf at the club. They learned how to maximize their playing time by planning ahead for their chores and assignments. The boys paid little attention to how good they had become and were getting better and better all along at playing golf.

Most often, they didn't even keep score because they knew they would never finish the round. Also, sometimes, depending on certain
"open holes," they would start playing in front of a group that had open holes in front of them.

Hummer was watching TV one evening at home, waiting for dinner, when his little sister said to him,

"If you ever need me to caddie for you in some match, I'd like to."

"That's nice of you Joanie, thanks, but there's practically no female caddies I know of."

"Well, anyway," she said, "I will do it if you want. Don't you remember that time I did it, and you won?"

"Sure do," answered Hummer.

"Maybe I bring you luck, like a lucky charm. Do you think I'm right?"

"Yes, I Sure do."

Hummer loved his job at the course, but even more, he loved playing golf. He was learning the art of exactly how to hit a golf ball and make it go high or low, turn left, or turn right, bounce and stop, or spin left, spin right, or spin straight back. These abilities, among other controls, including temperament, were all important and necessary to all professional golfers.

Hummer spent a lot of time practicing sand shots too. Sometimes he would hit 2 or 3 large buckets from the bunkers. He would create different lies to work with and learn from them. More importantly, to him, it was not a boring chore, but instead, he enjoyed it. He experimented with angles of attack, choke-down shots, and the like. He would practice abbreviated swings too. Chipping around the green with different lies took up a lot of his time. He even practiced the rarely used chop shot and added it to his abilities. He never ever felt any kind of doubt or waste of time while practicing. The repetition never bothered him either. No, he loved and enjoyed it all.

Nobody was keeping track of Hummer's practice times, not even him, but after nearly two complete seasons at Briar Lakes, Henry Muller had hit well over 500,000 golf balls, both playing and practicing there.

Hummer, at just seventeen, was already 6' tall. He had fairly wide shoulders with long muscular arms and wrists, he had strong legs with thighs like a young Jack Nicklaus, and he wore size 12 golf shoes. All of these dimensions were an advantage if properly used, if not used correctly, disaster was always 95% as to the result.

Yes, all of the ingredients were there, it was finding out how to put them all to good use with tempo and sync. That would be the challenge.

It is written somewhere, that: "Championship Chess is a physical game, and Professional Golf is a mental game." Jack Nicklaus has said the same thing numerous times.

It has been my experience that golf is a game of opposites, when driving off the tee, you aim right to go left, or you aim left to go right, etc.

# Chapter 3

In the Pro Shop one morning, while sitting at his desk reading the mail, the Pro was interrupted by one of his teenage employees.

"What is it, Mark?" asked the pro.

"I thought you might like to know; Hummer shot a 64 yesterday."

"What tees?" asked the pro.

"Back," answered the boy.

The Pro then put all the mail back into the in-box on his desk. He would read it later. He then asked Mark to tell Hummer he wanted to see him.

Ten minutes later, Hummer appeared at the door; "You wanted to see me?"

"Yes, I want to hear about your round yesterday."

"I had all of my chores done before we played," he answered.

"I am not asking about that. I'm asking about your round. Tell me about it."

"Oh, okay. It was a 64, I had eight birdies plus two lip-outs."

"What tees did you play from?"

"The Back ones. You know, the tips. We always play the back tees."

VISION 54
by Dudley Peters

"Listen, Hummer, I want you to tell me about your round, hole by hole. It is important for me to know all about this round."

"You mean Now?"

"Yes, right now, and don't leave anything out." He pulled up a chair.

"Okay, let me see. On the first hole, the par 5, I was in the greenside bunker with my second shot, then wedged it to one foot – tap-in birdie.

On two, I had a 9 iron in, which left me with a 14-footer, easy uphiller.

On three, I lipped out a 12-footer and only made par.

On four, I had a seven iron in, - 12 feet, left the birdie 2 inches short.

On five, with my second shot, I got on with a 4 iron, lipped out the eagle putt, and had a tap-in birdie.

At six, I spun my wedge in - stiff. Tapped it in for the easy birdie.

On seven, I took it around the corner and had a flip wedge, 6 feet, drained it. Then I two-putted both 8 and 9 for 31."

"Nice. You never used your eight-iron though, am I right?"

"I didn't have one. There wasn't one in the lost club bin. I only had eight clubs."

"What eight clubs?"

"Let's see; a 3 wood – 4 iron – 5 iron – 7 iron – 9 iron – sand wedge – wedge – putter."

"All from the bin?"

"Yeah, I can't afford to buy any, and neither can my parents. I just use what is in the bin. That's okay, right?"

"Sure, it's okay."

"Anything else?"

"Yes, the back nine, I need to hear about that too," said the Pro.

"I only had three birdies on the back, 12, 15, and 16. The rest were all pars. It was just a routine 33."

"Tell me anyway, no, wait, tell me how you birdied 15, what did you hit off the tee?"

"Okay, 15, the par three. Oh yeah, they had it set up at 188 yards, and the pin was back left on the third tier. I would have hit a 6 iron, but I didn't have one, so I hooded my 7, hooked it into about three feet, and the putt was dead straight."

"Anything else?"

"No, I'll talk to you later. Make sure the range ball machine is loaded."

*(The course record at Briar Lakes was 64, but it was not from the back tees.)*

VISION 54
by Dudley Peters

The pro was well aware of the fact that the course was not a severely hard challenge to shoot a low score, especially with a semi-tough course rating of 71.3 and a slope rating of 132. Even though, it does require a lot of skill to shoot a score of 64, after all, Briar Lakes was 35 years old, and the best score registered there was a 64 from the regular men's tees. It was the white tees, some 17 years ago.

At this youthful age, Hummer had developed a golf game and a swing to be envied.

The pro thought about all of this for a minute or so. Back tees, 64? Wow. No driver, someone's used clubs, and only eight of them. This is news; this is big news. Geeze, this 17-year-old kid could win on tour right now.

The pro thought to himself, I am going to personally Keep up with his scores from here on out, to keep myself more aware of his consistency. Plus, I think I'll take him with me to Bel-Aire Country Club for their annual Pro-Am event coming up. He then thought about Bel Aire being such a difficult golf course and quite a bit harder than Briar Lakes. This Pro-Am should be the perfect test to let me know just how good Hummer's current golf game really is.

A few minutes later the pro put in a call to the Bel-Aire Country Club, and he asked to speak to Steve Jennings, the head pro, who was hosting the Pro-Am event in two weeks. His call went to the answering machine.

## VISION 54
### by Dudley Peters

"Hey Steve, this is Brad Davis over at Briar Lakes, I am planning to play in the Pro-Am at your course. Please give me a call."

He got up and went to find Hummer to invite him. Hummer was getting a cart ready for the next user. He responded to Brad's question by saying, "Sure, I'd love to play, Thanks for asking me."

"Go get your favorite putter, I want to see it."

"I don't have one, I just use whatever I can find in the lost club bin."

"What type of putter do you like best of all?"

"Scotty Cameron 34-inch Phantom 5.5," was his answer.

"How do you know that?" asked the pro.

"Whenever I go to the Golf Superstore, I spend a lot of time on their artificial putting green and try out different putters. The Phantom 5.5 is my favorite."

"I am setting you up with a set of Titleist demo clubs. I need to know which ones you want, also I will get you that Cameron putter too. Any particulars with these new clubs?"

"Wow: If you're not kidding. Yes, I'd like a 9° Driver, a 15° 3 wood, and an 18° 5 wood. I need 4 through 9 metal shaft irons, stiff, a sand wedge, a pitching wedge, a 58° lob wedge, and maybe a nice little 20° rescue club too.  If that's not asking too much."

"I'll get them as soon as I can, hopefully, you can get in a few rounds with them before the Pro-am. Okay?"

"Boy, this is great, thanks."

Hummer thought to himself, I cannot believe it, this is so good, not only a new set of clubs, but I will have an opportunity to play in a Pro-Am with the Pro. I hope my game, or my nerves, do not let me down. Any screw-up I might make could be hard for me to handle. I feel like I have a good game, plus I'm anxious about having my own clubs. I cannot wait.

Even though Hummer's parents knew nothing about his golfing ability or his commitment to the game, they were in no way prepared for what lay ahead for their family, regarding their son Hummer and golf in the days to come.

Nobody could have dreamed it.

# Chapter 4

There were many, many, businessmen in the Rockville area that played golf and gambled on it also, sometimes making large bets among themselves. They were good at golf too, especially with the various handicaps they nurtured.

Some of the courses in the area were known for their members being heavy bettors. It was like a clique. If you had money, you could play in their groups. A typical round of golf with this clique might see players making bets of hundreds of dollars. Other players frequently would have one or two grand on the line. Sometimes, even more.

The club pros, everywhere in Maryland, were not allowed, by club rules, to engage in betting with any member or guest. This rule was rigorously enforced.

One of the money players was a good friend of Brad Davis, his name was Tim Parlette. Tim was 5 years older than Brad, but they have been friends for over 10 years.

They used to play golf against some heavy gamblers in money games. This was before Brad became the head pro at Briar Lakes, thus ending all that.

Brad made a lot of money from golf back then, along with Tim's 5 handicap and Brad at a 1, together, as a two-man team, they seldom lost.

by Dudley Peters

Tim had nerves of steel and wouldn't think twice about putting everything on the line at any time, he was one of those.

A threat to him, or an intimidation, was just another thrill to be added to the lengthy list of excitements he was always seeking and enjoyed. Both Tim and Brad made a formidable twosome and won a lot of money with their golf abilities during all those gambling years.

Even now, many, many times, Brad thought about giving up his job at Briar Lakes and getting back into gambling on golf. He had been making quite a lot more money in those gambling matches with his partner Tim, and it was much more fun back then. It was his wife that got him to stop and get a real job.

Tim still called Brad quite often to invite him to play in money games, but Brad had to refuse because of his title and commitment as a Country Club Head Pro. Tim would still call him, anyway, hoping Brad would accept.

Meanwhile, across town at the exclusive Woodcrest Golf & Country Club, Thomas Montclair, one of the many wealthy members and a high-stakes gambler, was playing gin rummy in the men's poker room and lounge. This was normal whenever it was raining, or for any other reason that the course was uninviting or closed.

Gambling can be, and is, very similar to drug addiction; it gets into yourblood, and addicts must gamble for the thrill of winning. If you lose, you just gamble on something else to keep the thrill (the high) alive. He was behind at the moment, losing to his opponent some $2,600 so far today. They had started playing at 10:30 AM, and it was now 2:30. Another Dewars' and water was delivered to him. He stirred it and took a sip. He drew a card from the deck and declared, "I'm knocking with two!" This was a typical day for him. Drinking and gambling, plus, it seemed that the more he drank, the luckier he got. He was one of those also. He gambled heavily on golf. He was just good enough to hold his own against any other golfer. He maintained a nine handicap. Of all his other faults, he had a few prominent things going for him.

He never cheated at golf, plus he was a good sport, both losing or winning, he was also a big tipper. This made him both likable and popular among the club members and staff.

In the Pro shop office at Woodcrest, Billy Jones, the head Pro was reading the invite sheet for the pro-am coming up at Bel-Aire Country Club next week. He filled out his invitation and e-mailed it in. One of the players he would be bringing with him was Thomas Montclair.

◇

Thomas Montclair was born into and grew up in a wealthy home. His father, John Montclair, owned a very successful commercial construction company. He built office buildings, airports, government buildings, and similar projects.

VISION 54
by Dudley Peters

His wife, Margaret, also came from a loaded family; she had only one sibling, a brother, one year younger than h

A year after marrying John, Margaret had serious trouble with the birth of Thomas and the result was that she would not have any more children, so Thomas was an only child.

Thomas, or Tommy as he liked to be called, took a liking to golf as a kid; he hung around the country club his father belonged to and simply charged everything he wanted onto his father's account. He developed a feeling of importance from doing that.

He took private lessons from the pro on a schedule that he often abused when he had other things he wanted to do. He had several girlfriends also, that kept him occupied and away from golf. Even so, his golfing ability was rather good but was not as sharp as needed in every category.

As a teenager, he had often observed older members making bets on the opening tee. He liked the idea of gambling on golf. Sure enough, one day, while he was on the putting green practicing, one of the older golfers called him over and asked if he could fill in for a member who couldn't make it in time to play. Tommy said, "Sure, and I want to be included in the bets too, if it's okay." He then told them, "My handicap is 7."

This day was the start of Tommy's golf gambling habit. He won $200.00 that day, and he was hooked; he was 18 years old at the time. That was 30 years ago. Tommy, right now, was very savvy and talented at gambling on golf. At 48 years of age, he carried a respectable 9 handicap.

When Tommy graduated from High School, he had an awfully tough time talking to his parents about not going to college. He eventually won out when both parents got tired of arguing about it.

Tommy was given a position in his father's company as a project coordinator. It took a while, but before long, he figured out a way to get out of daily work. He hired a young college graduate from OSU with a degree in business management. Bryson Redding was his name. Tommy gave him the title of co-coordinator. This proved to be a perfect cover. Thus, this arrangement allowed Tommy to show up at the office only rarely, and then, only when there was nothing going on that would prevent him from playing golf, gambling, or drinking.

He might as well not even have an office, but he did, and his co-coordinator learned to cover for him perfectly for years and years. This arrangement worked out beneficially for them both. Tommy made sure of that. Only once, early on, did Bryson cause Tommy to get reprimanded by his father.

That day, his father had come down to his office three separate times for a discussion about a certain project, only to find that Tommy was out for the day. Bryson failed to inform Tommy about this. His father sent a message that ordered Tommy to meet for a face-to-face at 8:30 the next morning, where Tommy received an old-fashioned chewing out.

The gist of the meeting was for him to get more involved in the company's business by spending more time overseeing projects.

"You need to be completely prepared to take over at any time, should some unforeseen events were to happen. Do you understand me?" "Yes."

When Tommy got back to his own office, he jumped all over Bryson. Threatened to fire him, "if anything like this ever happens again." He then added, "Why do you think I pay you so well?" Bryson apologized and said it would never happen again.

Tommy spent that entire day in his office. He was livid.

The next morning, Tommy came into his office again and looked over some of the projects currently under construction. After about two hours, he told Bryson that he was going out, but should be back later this afternoon. He didn't return. It would be some time before he showed up at his office again.

# Chapter 5

The phone rang in the pro shop. It was Steve Jennings returning Brad's call about the Pro-am tournament at Bel Aire Country Club.

"Hi, Steve. How are you doing?"

"Fine, but busy. How about you?"

"Good. I called to let you know I would like to play in Your Pro-Am again this year."

"Okay, sure. Are you coming alone?"

"No, I'm bringing this kid, Henry Mueller, with me to play."

"I hope he's a good golfer and that you are not just doing a favor for one of your regular members. How old is he, and is he any good?"

"He's 17. He carded a 64 yesterday here at Blair Lakes."

"Wow, from what tees?"

"The back ones."

"Bring him; I'll put you both with Thomas Montclair and Billy Jones. Billy's the head pro at Woodcrest."

"Sounds good, see you there. I must go now, Bye."

"Bye."

Brad then summoned Hummer. One of the employees there told him that Hummer was out on the course playing.

"Go get him."

A short time later, Hummer entered Pro's office.

"You wanted to see me?"

"Yes. Earlier this morning, I picked up your new clubs. You need to unbox them and put 'em into your new Bag along with this Scotty Cameron Phantom putter."

"Wow! I don't know what to say. Thank you, thank you very much. Geeze, when could I start using them?"

"Immediately. Why don't you finish your round with them right now? When you finish, take your bag into the pro shop, and put everything that you need in it to play golf. Don't worry about the cost. It's all covered."

"Okay, Thanks, this is great!"

"You know we have only nine days left before the Pro-Am."

"Okay; thanks again, thanks for everything. The clubs are nice, very nice."

"I hope you say that after you play with them."

"Don't worry."

He headed out to where his buddies were waiting for him. He took out his new driver and went to the tee, took six practice swings, and stepped up to the ball.

All of his buddies watched as Hummer connected.

VISION 54
by Dudley Peters

It was a mammoth-perfect drive over three hundred yards right down the middle.

His friends watched in awe and said so, after the shot. Hummer was not surprised, however. Because the club fit his stance and grip so perfectly and so effortlessly, his mind automatically had put his body and swing into perfect sync. The shot was pure.

Every one of the new clubs was ideal for him. He didn't keep score on the remaining holes. He just played with them and absorbed the feel of them. He started hitting extra shots, getting accustomed to the new feel and the new distances for each club. Hummer was happy. Very happy.

After the boys finished their game, they all went about getting their jobs done. After that, Hummer went to the putting green with a bucket of balls and started putting. He stayed there until almost total darkness set in. Hummer then went into the pro shop and filled up his new Titleist Cart Bag with his new clubs and other equipment needed to play Golf. Balls, Tees, Gloves, Markers, rain gear, rain Gloves, divot repair tool, Large Towel, Umbrella, Ball towel, Band-aids, Sun-block, Chap-stick, Ace bandage, Adhesive tape, Spike brush, bug spray, and Rules Book.

He returned the lost clubs he'd been using back into the bin. Then he went home.

The next morning, Brad found Hummer over at the ball machine, loading it up.

"How did the new clubs work for you?"

"They are just great, I love them. Thanks again."

"How far did you hit the Driver?" Brad asked.

"Long," answered Hummer.

During the next seven days, Hummer only managed to play three and a half rounds. He was starting to get a fairly good feel with the new clubs, but he wanted to play more than he did. He wanted to get well prepared for the Pro-Am Monday, but the course had a lot more than the normal amount of play by the members the entire week. This cost him to lose valuable practice time.

He brought his clubs home with him every single night. He would wash them, towel them off, rub them, and sight them, even if he hadn't used them. He would sit on the edge of his bed, and one by one, he would

place his hand grip on them, hold them straight out for a moment, then ease them back into the bag. He loved his new clubs. Joanie sees him in his room holding one. She leans in and asks, "Did you buy those new clubs?"

"No, they were given to me by Titleist."

"What? Why?" She asked.

"They are called demos, and Titleist is like a sponsor to me."

"They're new, right?"

"Yes, they are."

"I know you are playing in an important tournament tomorrow, right?"

"Yep, it's a Pro-Am Tournament at Bell Aire."

"I know where it is. I also know that you have to be rich to be a member there."

"I think so," he answered.

"Hummer, would you let me caddie for you tomorrow?"

"I don't think anybody is using a caddie for this one, but you are welcome to come with me as a spectator if you want."

"Oh yes, I'd like that; what time should I be ready to leave?"

"I'm supposed to meet Brad at 7:15 to help load up everything, so we need to leave here no later than 6:45."

"I'll be ready."

Hummer had picked up some old dog-eared magazines at the pro shop to bring home to read. He laid back on his bed, turned on the lamp, and started leafing through one when an article caught his attention. It was about the biggest event ever to have happened on the PGA Tour. It was quite interesting, mostly about winning a tournament with a miraculous hole-out for the victory and the like. An afterthought to the article was this question. It was posed to the top players on the PGA Tour.

*WHAT WOULD BE THE BIGGEST or GREATEST THING THAT COULD EVER HAPPEN IN PROFESSIONAL GOLF?*

There were only a few answers. The one that was mentioned most was a player Winning the US Open, winning the British Open, Winning the Masters, and winning the PGA Tournament, all in the same year, the "Grand Slam," is what it's called. Most of the top pros agreed.

Annika Sorenstam, deemed to be the best female golfer in the world at that time, did not agree, even though she admitted, "Winning the "Grand Slam, all 4 majors in a single year is truly a great feat, but it has already been done, Bobby Jones did it in 1930; In my judgment," She continued, "the greatest thing that could ever happen in golf would be *WHEN, AND IF, SOMEONE SHOOTS AT SCORE OF 54 ON A PAR 72 GOLF COURSE ON TOUR, 18 UNDER PAR."*

"I refer to it as my *Vision of a 54.* After all, winning the Grand Slam has already been done, but the '54' is still out there."

*Note: The lowest pro score of 58 was accomplished by Jim Furyk in 2016, but it was on a par 70 course. (12 under par.) Since 2010, there have been eight PGA Tour golfers who have shot a 59, including Jim Furik. He remains the only golfer to shoot a 58 on Tour, and he's the only golfer to break 60 twice. Bryson DeChambeau joined the 58 Club after his 12-nder round in a LIV*

VISION 54
by Dudley Peters

*Golf event. Feb 4, 2024, none of these scores were posted on a par 72 course.*

"54" is the equivalent of 18 BIRDIES, in 18 holes for 18 UNDER PAR IN ONE ROUND, ON A PAR 72. THAT WOULD BE IT, A "54."

Hummer looked up from the magazine, closed his eyes, and dreamed for just a moment that he was the player who did it. He quickly dispensed with this dream and went to sleep. Little did he know what the future held for him.

Nobody did.

# Chapter 6

The morning of the Pro-Am, Hummer was lying in his bed wide awake at five AM. His only thoughts were his new clubs and playing golf with the Pro at Bell Aire Golf Course.

He had never played there, or any other course. He just could not lay in bed anymore. He got up, went into the bathroom, and readied himself for the day. He was supposed to meet the Pro at seven-thirty to load up and head to the event. He and Joanie got there at ten after seven.

Brad asks Hummer, "Who is your friend?"

"Oh, this is my little sister Joanie."

"Hi Joanie, nice to meet you. Okay, let's load up and listen to me, Hummer. I do not want you to think about any sort of problems you might have with your game today; just relax and enjoy yourself. Let it come to you; do not chase after it. Okay?"

"I'll try to relax. I am so happy Joanie is here. She somehow always brings me luck."

They arrive at Bell Aire at 8:20, and registration opens at 8:30. Brad registers them both, and they receive their player's packet. Their tee time is 10:08 on hole number 1.

Hummer asked Brad what time he should start his warm-up routine. "I'd say around nine-thirty. Hummer had some time to spare, so he started looking around to see if he recognized anyone. Right about then, a man approached him and asked, "Are you the kid that Brad Davis entered to play today? The same kid that shot a 64 from the back tees at Briar Lakes two weeks ago?"

"Yes, I'm Henry Muller." He stuck out his hand.

"I'm Tommy Montclair, Henry; I'm pleased to meet you."

"Nice to meet you too, Mr. Montclair. Everyone calls me Hummer."

Okay, Hummer, it is."

"Thanks, this is my sister Joanie."

"Nice to meet you, Joanie. Say, Hummer, listen, I am playing with you today, and I am most interested in your golf game. I have been looking to sponsor a young, talented golfer for a couple of years now. You could be the one."

"I'm not sure what you mean."

"Well, if I see what I hope to see, we would enter into an agreement where I would pay you to play and practice golf every day for 2 years. I would pay all of your bills, all of your expenses, and whatever else necessary, so that you need only to concentrate on golf. It would be a 2-year gamble on my part. If it works or fails, there is no cost whatsoever to you."

"I'm not sure of what you're talking about, but, anyway, then what?"

"Well, it's like what I just told you: I pay all expenses for your playing and practicing golf, then when you start competing, should you were to qualify, or get accepted, to join up with any of the accredited Pro Golf Circuits, during this time, then we would make out a legal contract whereas I would own 18% of the franchise."

"Sounds good, but I would need to ask my Pro, Brad Davis, about this. I'm sorry, but I don't know anything about what you're talking about."

"Okay, Sure. But, before any of this could happen, I must see you play and see how you hold up under pressure. Plus, I'm most interested in your score. You know what I mean?"

"Oh, okay. It all sure sounds good to me."

"Oh, there is one more thing. If you were to somehow make it into the big show, the PGA Tour, then we would make out a new contract whereby I would still pay the bills, but I would then own 22% of the franchise."

"Mr. Montclair, I – "Call me Tommy, please."

"– Okay Tommy, it all sounds good to me, but I need to think about all this. I need to talk with my pro. I believe I'm already starting to feel what golf pressure might be like."

It was now 9:25, and Hummer and Joanie headed to the practice range. Joanie was carrying his bag.

by Dudley Peters

Hummer found an open space. He started his routine with his 8-iron. He hit 8 balls. Only 1 person was watching him: his little sister Joanie. He asked for his 6-iron, and Joanie fumbled around and found it. She handed it to him, then she took back the 8-iron, cleaned it, and put it back into the bag. After he worked all the irons, he brought out the driver.

All of the people around the practice range heard it, including Tommy Montclair. It was the percussion of the hit. All heads turned at the same time, all looking at the kid that just hit a practice ball over the fence some 310 yards away.

When Hummer and Joannie, still carrying his bag, left and went to the practice green, there were spectators following. They watched him putt. It was now 5 minutes until his tee time.

Brad asked Hummer, "Is Joanie caddying for you today?"

Hummer thought for 1 second and replied, "Absolutely."

"Well, Hummer, I want to introduce you to Pro Billy Jones."

Billy stuck out his hand, and Hummer shook it.

"Nice to meet you," Hummer said.

"This is my golfing buddy, Tommy Montclair."

"We have already met," said Hummer.

"Oh, great! Play well." He went back to practice his putting.

## VISION 54
### by Dudley Peters

Tee time arrived. In the foursome were the two club Pros, plus Tommy and Hummer. When they were given the green light, Hummer asked, "You want me to hit first?"

The #1 hole was a par 4, - 428 yards in length.

Brad answered, "No. I would like you to hit fourth."

Billy tees up his ball and hits a nice drive 250 yards into the fairway. Tommy hooked his drive into a fairway bunker, and Brad hit a nice drive just off the fairway onto the first cut, which is about 245 yards. Hummer selected his driver and smashed one all the way down, to just 60 yards short of the green.

The two Pros and Tommy turn and just look at each other. "Nice shot," somebody said, and they were off.

There was no doubt Hummer was the one in the spotlight. Yes, he birdied the first hole, but at the end of the front nine, Hummer had carded a one-over par, 37. He double-bogeyed #5 after hitting into the water, then bogeyed both #7 and #8 with lip outs. He had only 3 birdies.

Tommy asked Hummer, "Have you ever played here before?"

"No, the only golf course I've ever played is Briar Lakes."

"Wow. I didn't know that," said Tommy

Hummer's foursome encountered a backup on the #10 tee. While they were waiting, Brad went over and talked to Hummer in a low, serious voice;

"Look at me," he waited until he gets his complete attention, then said, "do you remember me telling you not to chase it, just let it come to you?"

"Yes, I do, but both of those lip-outs could have dropped."

"Don't worry about the game behind you. Always play the game in front of you. Okay? Please remember that."

"Okay."

These pro-ams usually do not draw a lot of spectators, even though there's no attendance fee for spectators. It's normal to have around 80 to 100 or so golf fans attending, plus one or two golf reporters. The Tee box at #10 finally opened up, and they prepared to start the back nine. There was a small spectator group, about 12, that had been following them for the first nine. A few had left to go watch other groups play, but as the back nine started unfolding, the small group became a crowd.

The four players, Joanie, plus the crowd, all watched in amazement as Hummer scored seven birdies and 2 pars for a smooth, record-tying 29 on the back nine.

When all the scores were in, Hummer had won the Pro-Am by 3 shots. One of the two sports reporters there, Benny Devine, found Hummer and did a short interview with him.

Tommy Montclair saw everything he needed to see. He was captivated. No, more than that. He was excited, very excited. He knew he had something. Something powerful that he could make money with,

something that would only get better, something he could earn respect with, something that would help support his gambling, and something to get him some much sought-after and needed notoriety and praise.

Tommy Montgomery was excited and eager.

# Chapter 7

The next day, just after the Pro-am, Tommy called Hummer on his cell phone and asked him if he could play a round of golf tomorrow at one o'clock.  It would be at his home course, Woodcrest. Hummer answered, "Sure, of course, I would. I'll just tell Brad I can only work the morning shift. There should be no problem."

"Great! Come early, so we can have lunch. Okay?"

"Sure."

"Good, but Hummer, I need to let you know something: it will be a money match."

"Ut-oh. I don't know about that, Tommy. I can't afford to gamble or lose any money."

"Oh, Hummer, let me tell you; It's not a gamble for you. You can't lose, you can only win. I pay for any and all losses. Period," he said.

"Should we win, however, you get two grand."

"What? You're kidding, right?" asked Hummer. "Two thousand dollars?"

"No, I'm not kidding," said Tommy.

"Can I ask how much we, uh, you, will be playing for?"

"Sure, there will be between 10 and 15 grand on the line with these guys."

*There is an overwhelming amount of gambling going on at any and all golf courses in the US. The more money the players have, the more money they risk. Because of various situations, amateurs have to deal with their ability to play and gamble. Some depend on a partner to make it a better chance  to win. Pick up the slack. So to speak.*

*There are more ways to gamble on golf than any other sport. Later in this book, I have listed some of them. You might find one that you like.*

Wednesday morning, Hummer gets to work a little earlier than normal and gets his chores squared away. He was thinking all night about the two thousand dollars he could win. Even now, he was still thinking about what to do with it, should he win. It was a nice thing for a teenager to think about. His mind was rambling, and he was getting anxious.

The next morning, while eating cereal, he told Joanie about the offer, he asked her about what to do with any money he might win. She answered, "If it was me, I'd open a savings account and put it there. How much are we talking about?"

"Yeah, thanks, that's a good idea. Uh, two thousand," he told her. Joanie looked at him but said nothing.

by Dudley Peters

One of his buddies, John, drove him to Woodcrest CC. He got there at 11:30. Dropped his bag at the bag drop and informed the attendant he would be playing with Mr. Montclair, who had a one O'clock tee time.  He then thanked John for the lift.

"Are you going to need a ride home later?"

"I don't know. I'll call you if I do. Okay?"

"Sure, Good Luck."

Just then, Tommy appeared out of nowhere.

"Glad you're here," he said. "How did you get here anyway?"

"My buddy John Coates brought me. He has his own car."

"I wasn't thinking Hummer, I should have sent my driver to get you. Sorry about that."

"That's okay."

"Come on, let's go eat."

They went into this elegant, Brass-clad, Cherry Wainscot-paneled grille room, where they got a table and ordered lunch. Hummer asked, "Who are we playing against?"

"Doctor Frank Goulami and Jack Korman."

How good are they?"

"Doc's a 9 handicapper, and Jack used to be a club pro before he got his amateur status back. He's a 2 right now."

"Wow, it sounds like we have our hands full."

"Naw, they're both losers. They think they're better than they are."

Just then, both men came over to Tommy's table. Shook hands with everybody and briefly sat down. Doc asked, "What's the kids' handicap?"

"Zero," answered Tommy.

"Nice, how about a friendly game today, say a 5 grand Nassau, automatic 2 down presses, and 25-dollar trash? Me and Jack against you and the kid?"

Tommy spoke up, "Call him Hummer Please. It sounds much better than Kid."

Doc said, "Sure, but Let me ask you something, looking at Hummer, have you ever played here before?"

"No, not yet. Today will be my first time."

He looked back at his partner Jack. He raised his eyebrows. Doc then said, "Say, Tommy, let's make that a 7 grand Nassau, what do you say?"

"You got it. See you out there."

Tommy and Hummer won a close and exciting match that could have gone either way. Hummer wound up shooting 70, just two under par, but he did win several holes during the round and kept the bet close. It was Tommy (getting a stroke) sinking a twenty-footer on the last hole that clinched the win. Hummer collected his 2 grand via a check, written right then, in the clubhouse.

Tommy had already decided that any and all money Hummer would get from their agreement would be by way of a paper trail.

All four of the players sat around the grill room talking golf. Tommy had two Dewars and water, Hummer had a grilled cheese sandwich and one beer.

The next day, Joanie and Hummer opened a savings account at the local bank under both their names.

More money games followed. Hummer starts piling up cash. He decides not to tell anyone about how much money he has accumulated in the account, he also asks Joanie not to tell anyone.

They played several more times together during the rest of the summer, right up to the time Hummer started back to High School for his senior year. He would be turning 18 next April.

Hummer now had just over $14 thousand in his savings account. He and Tommy had won 7 times in the 9 matches they played.

After their last match, Tommy recognizes what he now has in Hummer. In the nine matches, plus the Pro-am, he saw more than he hoped for. This kid had it. The ability to play golf at a high level without any uncertainty or fear. Hummer's phone goes off, it's Tommy:

"Hi Tommy, what's up?"

VISION 54<br>
by Dudley Peters

"Bad news, I fractured a bone in my left wrist today. My Doctor said it would be probably six weeks before I could play golf again."

"Wow, that is bad news. How did it happen?"

"I was in my garage checking degree angles on my irons when I tripped and fell hard onto the concrete. My left hand and wrist took the blow."

"Sorry to hear this."

"I know you are doing pretty well with our deal, but now we must put that on the back burner. If you need any money, just let me know."

"Thanks, Tommy."

# Chapter 8

Tim Parlette also had heard about the 64 Hummer carded at Briar Lakes a month ago, so he called his old gambling partner, Brad Davis, to ask about this kid who shot the 64. He wanted to know if he had nerves enough to play under the pressure of a big bet.

Brad told him that he took Hummer with him to play in the Pro-am at Bell Aire Country Club and added, "The pressure of playing in a pro-am with spectators watching didn't bother him in the least. He shot 37 on the front, then carded a record-tying 29 on the back nine."

"Sounds like a 66; you're not kidding, right?" and added, "did he win it?"

"Yes, he won it, he won by 3 shots, and no, I'm not kidding, but you need to know a few things. As of today, Bell Aire Country Club is the only other golf course he has ever played, but then, right after that, he played Woodcrest, making them the only three courses he has ever played, and those two, only once. There's a chance that he might have played some other course on the two days he took off from work too. I'm not sure about that."

"What? What do you mean?"

"I mean, just what I said."

"What did he shoot at Woodcrest?"

"I don't know right now. All I know is that he won."

"Do I have your permission to ask him if he would like to play as my partner for some good heavy action?"

"Sure, but it would be up to you to get him to say okay."

"Do you have his cell number?"

"Yes, I'll text it to you."

"Thanks."

# Chapter 9

Hummer was home, cleaning his clubs, awaiting dinner, when his cell went off. It was a call from the son of one of the wealthy heavy gamblers at Woodcrest Country Club, Adam Schrager IV.

"Hey Hummer, This is Adam Schrager, you played golf with my father a couple of times this summer. I believe that we are the same age. I graduated from Bethesda High School last year, I just turned 19."

"Hi Adam, yes, your Dad, Mr. Schrager, is a very good golfer, plus he treated me nicely, and he's a gentleman. What's up?" He asked.

"Okay; What I'm calling about is that I have a match lined up over at Columbia Country Club that we, you and me, could more than likely win. It's with two guys our age who are good golfers and love gambling on golf. I figure we could merge in with them and later, other players around our age. We could win some money and have fun doing it. What do you say?"

"First of all, said Hummer. I'm still in high school. I'm only 17. I'll be 18 next April. Playing golf is what I like to do best of all. Gambling on it is something I've never done."

"What are you talking about? My father is one of the biggest golf gamblers at Woodcrest. You and Tommy were gambling then."

"No, not me. Just Tommy."

"Oh, What? I didn't know that, but anyway, there are plenty of guys our age who are into gambling on golf. I feel certain we can do pretty well. My dad told me about you and your golf game. As for myself, I'm pretty good at it too. I carry a 7 handicap. So, what do you think?"

"How much will it cost for me to play?"

"Both our opponents' parents are members there, but to answer your question, nothing. We will be their guests."

"How much do I need to gamble with?"

"Our first match, we will probably have five hundred on the line. Let's see how we do. After that, we can change the amount we bet."

"When do you want to do this?" asked Hummer.

"What are you doing tomorrow?"

"What time?"

"They already have a tee time at 1:08," said Adam.

"I'll call you back in five minutes."

"Okay."

Hummer took this time to think about what to do. With Tommy injured, he believed this might be a timely invitation. He called him back.

"Can you pick me up at "Briar Lakes?"

"Sure, I'll be there around ten thirty. Look for me, I'll be driving a new, cherry red Wrangler Sport."

"You caught me in a good frame of mind. I'm not working anyway, Briar Lakes is closed tomorrow, they're aerating the greens, so, I'll see you tomorrow."

"Okay, bye."

The next morning, right after breakfast, Hummer rode his bike to the bank and withdrew $1,000, then put it into his wallet. He then peddled over to the golf course. It was only ten o'clock, so he checked his bag for things he needed for today's match. When he was satisfied, he just started re-cleaning his clubs and his shoes.

Adam pulled in just before ten-thirty, they met for the first time, shook hands, and then loaded up. They pulled up to the guardhouse. Adam gave the guard his name and then drove around to the bag drop. It was now 11:05. One of the uniformed attendants grabbed the two bags out of the back.

Hummer said to Adam, "This is some swanky place."

"Yes. They like it this way: everything is way overdone and snobbish. You know what I mean?"

"Yeah."

"Hummer, are you ready for this, your first gambling venture?"

"I'm good," he said as they were tying up their golf shoes.

"You Sure?" asked Adam.

"Yeah, I'm ready," said Hummer.

*Hummer had now made a decision to gamble his own money on a golf match. Usually, gambling on golf is not devastating, but sometimes it can lead to total devastation.*

"Com-on, let's go find our two friends."

"We will share a caddie unless you want one for yourself. Caddies are required here."

"Okay then, let's just share one."

Adam goes over to the caddy shack and lines up the caddy.

"Let's go get a quick bite. Larry and Mike are probably in there waiting for us."

In the men's grille, all of the employees were dressed in black tuxedo-like uniforms. They go over to the table, and Adam said, "Hey guys, This is my partner, Hummer Muller. Hummer, meet Larry Eul and Mike Castelli. They're both 3 handicappers."

They all stood up, and everybody shook hands.

"What is your handicap?"

"I'm still a 7, and Hummer is scratch," Adam answered.

"Yes. Well, it sounds like a good, tough match to me," said Larry.

After a quick lunch, they started warming up on the range, Hummer didn't try to show off by hitting some mammoth drives; he did, however, bring out his driver, swing it a few times, but then put it back. He never hit a ball with it while on the range.

He hit several long shots with his 3 wood. When they all were on the putting green, Larry asked Hummer if he had ever played here Before. No, was his answer.

In an attempt to cause worry, Mike said, "It takes a while to get used to these extremely fast greens here."

"I played some really fast greens a couple of weeks ago," Hummer responded.

Their tee time arrived, and the starter informs them, they have to start on #10. "No problem," said Larry. While on the tee, Mike then said, "How about a two hundred dollar Nassau with automatic two-down presses? Larry and I get 3, and Adam gets 7 all day?"

"You got it," answered Adam.

"What about trash?"

"Let's do Greenies only, but on all 18 holes, 10 dollars each."

Larry throws up a tee, it points toward Adam.

"Okay Adam, you have the honors. Hit away."

The #10 hole at Columbia is a par 4, some 430 yards long, slightly bent to the left but still almost straight. You can see the green from the tee. There's a small pond in front of an elevated green, the distance to the pond is 365 yards from the back, Blue tees, where they were.

by Dudley Peters

"Let me hit first Hummer, I'm ready." Adam hits a nice drive to the edge of the fairway about 245 yards out.  Hummer tees up his ball and asked, "How much is it to the water?"

"Water? Don't worry about it. It's at least 360 or 370 yards from here," answered Adam.

"Yeah, but it's a little bit downhill, isn't it? I better hit the 3 wood."

Larry, Mike, and Adam all looked at each other with their eyebrows crunched together.  Hummer stepped up and connected. The ball flew high and long. It came to rest 310 yards down the line. Adam said, "Nice drive, partner."

"Thanks," said Hummer, "for a minute there, I thought I was in the lake," and they were off.

At the end of the front nine, it proved to be a tough competitive match. Adam and Hummer were 1 up on the Nassau, and they were also 6 up in the trash bet. Mike asks if anyone wants something from the grille room. They got two sodas and two iced tea and lemonade and some peanut butter & cheese crackers.

When they got around to the #1 tee, there was no adjustment made regarding the bets. Adam and Hummer held the honors. Adam teed his ball up, and then Mike said let's make a $200 side bet on the back nine, best ball gross, no press. You got it, answered Adam.

VISION 54
by Dudley Peters

There was a total of 6 birdies made on the front nine; Hummer had 3 of them.

When the match ended, Adam and Hummer won the Nassau 3-ways. (the front nine and the middle. The back nine was halved.) There were no presses earned. They also won $60 trash. The $200 side bet was halved.

All in all, it was a really close match and very enjoyable for all four players. So, on Hummer 's first time gambling on his golf ability, with his own money, he won $660.00 he felt good. He liked it. It was anything but devastating. It was all sugar plums, candy, and cake. He enjoyed it a lot.

He felt good. He was on cloud nine. The future looked extremely bright for now.

# Chapter 10

Meanwhile, something was going on across town at the sports desk of the Post Newspaper. Benny Devine, one of the sportswriters who had covered the Bel Aire Pro-Am and witnessed the 29 scored by Hummer that day on the back nine, which led to his win by three strokes, decided to write a column about the Tournament and the winner, Hummer Mueller.

He wrote a summary of his interview and what he had witnessed. A teenager with no findable record, or knowledge about his golf prowess provided a show of golf expertise for those spectators who were there to witness it.

Benny wrote that what he saw before the start, out at the driving range, got his immediate attention. This young kid could really hit a golf ball high and long, really high and really long. Again and again, he would hi-fly the ball over 300 yards in the air out over the fence at the back of the range. This alone drew a crowd of watchers, he wrote.

Then, after carding a one over par on the front nine at Bell Aire, Henry Muller, then roused everyone by rattling off seven birdies and two pars, to tie the course record of 29 on the back nine. The 66 earned him a 3-stroke victory over local club pros and other veteran players.

Henry was interviewed by a second reporter, Jesse Grant, after the win. Jesse found out that Hummer likes to be called by his nickname.

"Hummer."

When Hummer was asked, "How did you do it, did you know the course that well, or what?"

He told Jesse, "This is not only my first time playing Bell Aire Country Club, but also my first time to play any organized golf event anywhere."

"Are you telling me that this is the first time that you have ever played in a golf tournament?"

"Yes."

"This is remarkable."

"Do you have any plans for future tournaments?"

"I don't know."

Tommy Montgomery read the article along with many golf enthusiasts. Tammy called Hummer and told him that he liked the article about him. Hummer also got a few other calls from friends.

# Chapter 11

School was about to start. For Hummer, it would be his senior year. He was home when his mother asked him what he needed in the way of clothes for school. She reminded him she would only be buying the necessities. Money was tight right now, she said.

Hummer tells his mother that he will pay for all of the clothes for both him and Joanie. She said, "You saved some money this summer?"

"Yes."

"That's very sweet of you Honey, I'm so glad you saved it. Every little bit helps."

After dinner, Joanie and Hummer went to the mall, and they both picked out some school clothes they wanted. Hummer paid with cash. Joanie asks about an outfit she really liked, but it was costly, plus she needed certain shoes to go with it. Hummer told her, go get it. Joanie was elated. They both were ready and anxious for the new school year.

Hummer felt really good; things were going well, and it was all visions of glory and fun, as far as he could see. Tomorrow would be the first day of School; It would be Hummer's senior year.

There was this one particular girl at school that he especially liked. Her name was Amanda Sheridan. He had spoken to her a few times last year and had traded notes, although he never got her phone number. Also, they never went out on a date or to a movie together.

Often, during the long summer season, when Hummer was working at the golf course, he would think about her. He was hoping that she would be returning for her senior year. He feared the possibility that her parents might have moved away and he would never see her again. They didn't.

Hummer could have never imagined the disaster that awaited the two of them. On the first day of school, Amanda came to his locker and asked to borrow his jacket to wear. He was elated about this; It was a good sign for sure. It turned out that they were even scheduled to have three classes together, and Hummer was pleased. At the end of the day, Amanda returned his jacket, thanked him, and ran off with some other girls.

Hummer knew that notes were often intentionally left in pockets of borrowed jackets. He felt it in the right pocket, pulled it out, and read it.

Thank you for lending me your jacket, we should get together sometime. Plus, her phone number was included.

A short moment later, he felt the other pocket, and in there he found a small plastic bag with two pills inside. Also, another note from Amanda reads: Hummer, make sure to keep this to yourself. These are the best I've ever tried. Only take one of these, where no one can see you, and don't tell anyone. Love Amanda.

VISION 54
by Dudley Peters

This note left him stunned. His heart skipped a beat as he read the note, his mind swirling with confusion and disbelief. He had never expected Amanda to leave such a message for him, let alone one encouraging drug use. He couldn't believe it. He read it again.

A wave of disappointment washed over him, and the image of the girl he had admired started to blur as he stood there, clutching the note in his hand. A mixture of emotions flooded his mind. A very small tinge was sensed by him, with the intrigue of the idea of experiencing something new, something that could potentially create a bond between him and Amanda. Another part, reality, however, whispered caution and warned him of the dangers that lurked within the small plastic bag.

Hummer took a deep breath and closed his eyes, struggling to make sense of it all. He knew there had to be a decision made regarding just how to handle this unexpected and unpleasant surprise.

The words on the note replayed in his mind, each syllable searing into his conscience. *"The best I've ever tried,"*-*"where no one can see you." - "Don't tell anyone."* He felt a chill run down his spine as the reality of the situation sunk in. He knew that unwanted, serious trouble had now entered his short relationship with Amanda and himself.

by Dudley Peters

The girl he admired was involved in something far darker than he had ever imagined. The weight of the decision bore down upon him,

Hummer knew he had to make a choice. A choice that could define not only his own future but also his relationship with Amanda. He might succumb to the temptation and delve into the unknown, or he could rise above it and confront her about the troubling message.

Driven by a sense of responsibility instilled by his family upbringing, Hummer crumpled the note in his hand, determined to find the intent behind Amanda's actions. The next day, Amanda showed up at his locker to borrow his jacket again. Hummer, before handing over his jacket, said to her, "Amanda, I'm going to need to discuss with you the note you left for me yesterday."

"Okay," she answered.

"Amanda," he began, his voice low and tense.

"About your note. I need to know what's going on. Why would you suggest something like that? We barely know each other; I like you, and I believe that you like me, too, but we're not going steady or anything. At least not right now."

Amanda's eyes widened with a mix of surprise and guilt. She shifted uncomfortably, unable to meet Hummer's gaze. After a moment of silence, she finally spoke, her voice tinged with vulnerability.

"I'm sorry, Hummer. I didn't mean for it to get you upset. I thought... I thought it would be just a joke. I never dreamt you would take it so seriously."

Hummer's heart sank at her response, realizing that she had underestimated the consequences of her actions.

"This is not a joke, Amanda. Drugs are serious, and I sure hope that you never go down this path."

With her voice barely a whisper, she said, "You are so right. I just wanted to get your attention. I'm sorry."

As they stood there, the weight of their unspoken emotions hung in the air. Hummer couldn't help but feel a small sense of relief come over him after Amanda apologized.

He knew he had made the right decision in confronting her, but he also couldn't help but feel a twinge of disappointment. He had hoped that his feelings for Amanda could have blossomed into something more, but now he realized that there were problems here. There might be even more problems with Amanda than he had thought or met the eye.

She stopped asking for his jacket. Over the next few days, Hummer watched as Amanda distanced herself from the crowd that had previously surrounded her. He saw her once sitting alone during lunch, her eyes cast down as she silently ate her food. He sometimes caught her staring off into space, lost in thought, and wondered if she, too, was grappling with the same internal struggles that he had been experiencing regarding her.

Hummer approached Amanda as she sat on a bench with two of her girlfriends. They were laughing and talking. He sat down beside her and asked, "Hi, girls, what are you talking about that's so funny?"

"Hi Hummer, this is Shirley and Kim. We're just taking in some sunshine."

"Good for you."

Amanda said, "Kim is having a pool party Saturday night at her parents' house. Would you like to join us?"

"Sounds like fun. Who's going to be there?"

Kim said, "Everybody, I've got the whole house to myself. My parents are away this weekend. It'll be starting around 6:30 or 7 PM."

"Thanks for the invite; I'll let you know."

"You don't need to let me know. Just come if you can; if you do come, bring your swimsuit, bring some beer, or whatever," said Kim.

Hummer asked Amanda if he could talk to her for a minute. They went over to a vacant bench.

"Are you okay?" He asked.

## VISION 54
### by Dudley Peters

"Yes, I'm fine."

"I'm really glad to hear that. Getting caught up in drugs and pills is like playing with dynamite. It can ruin a person's life. As for me, I'll never do drugs, and I don't smoke either. The only bad habit I have is that I like beer. To me, beer is something I think most anyone can handle without major complications. I'm sure about that." (Hummer *could not have been more wrong.*)

"I'll tell you something hard to believe. I actually think that a couple of beers makes me play better golf. It's happened several times while I was playing with Mark," he said.

"Only once did I make the mistake of drinking too much beer; I was playing golf with my buddies on a slow day at the course. Mark had brought a cooler full of Miller Light with him and put it in his cart. It was a hot and humid day, and I drank way too many beers. I suddenly felt a little woozy. Sure enough, I wrecked one of the golf carts. But drugs, no way. I will never make the mistake of using drugs."

"I heard that beer is just as bad as hard liquor," she spoke.

"Naw. That's not true. I can handle beer."

"Well, maybe I can handle things too, as long as I don't overdo it. I have to go home now; my mother is waiting for me. We're supposed to go to the mall. Scc ya."

She got up and went back to the bench where her girlfriends were. Hummer felt like he just got hit by a baseball bat. He couldn't believe what he had just heard. He knew that he had to do some heavy thinking about all this and just what it all meant.

# Chapter 12

Hummer receives a call from Tommy, who tells Him he wants him to qualify for the US Amateur Championship to be held next fall.

"I'll provide the expenses as well as a dietician and trainer coach for you. I'll get all of the information we need and get back to you. What do you think?"

"Sounds good to me, but you know School has already started, and I'm in school right now. My senior year."

"That should be no problem; it's only a one-day qualifier."

"I can't say right now, but I might be able to do it. When and Where is it?"

"As far as where we have a choice, I think Richmond Country Club, down in Richmond, will be our best choice. The when part is pretty soon; I will find that out today, I hope."

"Have you mentioned any of this to Brad?"

"No, but I'm on my way to meet him right now."

"Good. If I were to qualify, where and when is the main event held?"

"It's going to be at Cherry Hills Golf Club, Cherry Hills, Colorado."

"Wow! Do you know the dates yet?"

"No, not right now, but I do know it's next September. I will get all of the information we need on the qualifier and let you know."

"Okay. Sounds great."

*The United States Amateur Championship, commonly known as the U.S. Amateur, is the leading annual golf tournament in the United States for amateur golfers. It is organized by the United States Golf Association. It is currently held each year over a 7-day period, usually in September.*

*All across the nation, over 8,000 amateur golfers, as well as amateurs from other countries, will sign up to earn a playing slot in the US Amateur.*

*After one day of qualifying at selected golf courses across the country, there will then be 312 players that advance. At this point, the US Amateur tournament will consist of two days of stroke play for the 312 players, with the leading 64 competitors moving on. Then, a knockout competition is held at match play to decide the champion. All knockout matches are over 18 holes except for the final, which consists of 36 holes, separated into morning and afternoon 18-hole rounds.*

*Nowadays, it is usually won by players in their late teens or early twenties who are working towards a career as a tournament professional.*

The next day, Tommy called Hummer and said, "There are 5 qualifying courses within a reasonable driving distance for us. We can pick one from that list. We have plenty of time. This qualifier is thirteen days away, one week from this Friday."

"Okay," he said.

"I know that you have never played any of these 5 courses, so I will obtain a scorecard from each one and get them to you for your review."

"Yeah, that would be nice."

"Your Pro, Brad, will have the cards in hand as soon as I get my hands on them."

"Thanks, Tommy."

"You're welcome. This will be the start of your golfing career," he blurted out. "You're the man. No, wait, you're my man."

(Note:) Hummer *had a circumstance that had crept up on him, which he paid no attention to. He had developed a likeness for beer. This was the type of thing that could bring about a serious, troubling condition down the road if he wasn't careful. He deliberately kept this information away from Tommy Montgomery. He thought it best not to mention it to anyone. He knew he could handle it. It would never become a problem. He thought.*

*His golfing buddies got him started on it, and he liked it. At seventeen, he became a beer drinker; However, it didn't seem to interfere with his golfing ability, not yet anyway, and no one said anything. After all, he wasn't a guzzler, at least not yet.*

The next morning, Hummer hurried over to the course and retrieved the 5 scorecards of the courses that were hosting the qualifying rounds for the US Amateur Tournament. He got them and then went into the Pro's office and took a seat. Brad had not come in yet.

When Brad came in, Hummer was looking at the scorecard yardages on the holes at each course.

"How ya doing?" asked the Pro.

"I'm fine, thanks. I need to decide which course I should play to try to qualify for the US Amateur," answered Hummer.

"I went over the cards yesterday myself. I thought you should go to The Country Club of Richmond and qualify there," Brad said.

"Okay," said Hummer, "but why there?"

"You could overpower that course. You could own it. I wanted you to play it twice, one week before the qualifier and once with me. I would be setting that up for us."

"Okay."

# Chapter 13

Brad called Hummer and told him the dates of the two practice rounds at Richmond. Brad also said that he would play mainly to observe dangerous situations on certain holes in case any changes needed to be made regarding strategy, layups, and the like. Hummer asked Brad if Joanie could come along. Brad said, sure, she could; he wasn't carrying his clubs.

"Thanks, Brad."

"Listen, Hummer: This is serious stuff; I can't emphasize this enough. This golf event is life-changing if you were to win the US Amateur Open. But first, we must qualify here next weekend." He then said, "We're going to make this happen, but only one day at a time."

"I'll do my best; I am playing pretty well right now."

"There's one more thing. A clear mind! You cannot have any worrisome thoughts lingering in your head. You must have a clear mind to win. Your competitors will be fully prepared and skilled. I'm only asking you this because I want you to succeed and have everything needed to get there. So, Let me ask you, do you have a clear mind right now?"

"I think I'm okay, but I do have a nagging situation going on right now with my girlfriend."

"How bad is it?"

"Really bad, but I believe she's working through it right now."

"Should I know what it is?"

"There will be no need. I have been thinking about getting out of our relationship for a while. I decided to break it off with her properly and do it right away. I know it's the right thing for both of us to do. I just know it. Thanks, Brad; my answer is that I definitely will have a clear mind right away.  I'll be ready to play."

The next day the weather forecast called for rain, and rain it did. The two days that Hummer was to practice with Brad were rained out. Thus, the all-important practice plans were canceled. Brad was quite upset about this. He knew the importance of course knowledge was now lost for Hummer.

The day before the tournament, Hummer's phone went off; it was Tommy Montclair.

"Hey Hummer, how are you feeling?"

"Pretty good, thanks."

"I know you're ready for tomorrow, but I'm wishing you luck anyway. Do you want to ride with me?"

"Oh, no thanks, I'm riding down with Brad. Thanks anyway."

"No problem, see you in Richmond." Tommy decided not to tell Hummer, but he had placed a few bets, totaling twenty thousand dollars on him, to qualify for the Tournament.

# Chapter 14

<u>Qualifying for the US Amateur Championship:</u>

Hummer was going over the yardages on certain holes on the scorecard. He was firstly looking for any par 4s that he could drive. He saw that there might be two that were possible, #8 and #11; they were both dogleg holes. He could hit his ball over the trees and cut off the dogleg yardage, maybe. He was also looking at the ranking of the holes.

Joanie poked her head in and asked if she could bring one of her girlfriends with her to the tournament. Hummer said, "Sure, that's no problem, but you might have to drive yourself. I'm not sure what Brad has planned for the two of us."

"That's okay; Mom and Susan are coming too; we're riding with them."

<u>THE ROUND:</u>

When Hummer showed up at the golf course to prepare himself for this important day. A day of competition for an elusive playing slot in the US Amateur Open. No one there paid any attention to him; after all, he was just another nobody. He went totally unnoticed, like most of the other young players there. His entry ticket and ID were in the lanyard around his neck. A tournament official checked him through the gate, and he carried his own clubs and a utility bag with him into the locker room. Almost all of the players were college boys, and most of them were on the college golf team at their various schools. There were some older players there, plus there were also amateur players from all over the world who were eligible to compete for the two slots, going to the two lowest scores of the day. Thus, qualifying for one of the 312 playing slots required to be filled for the start of the upcoming US Amateur Open.

Hummer's tee time was two hours away. He readied himself and headed out to the range. As expected, every space had been reserved; he finally found the one with his name on it and started his warm-up routine.

A fairly large crowd was observing other players at the range hitting balls. Hummer then started his warm-up routine, swinging and hitting his irons, but no one was watching him, that is, until he picked up his driver and hit it.

The ball went so high and so far that even some of the players on the range stopped and looked around to see who had hit that practice drive out over and beyond the 300-yard marker sign. A sizable portion of observers moved into position to see him better. They watched in amazement as Hummer hit several more mammoth drives.

He left the range 30 minutes before his tee time. He went straight to the practice putting green. He went through his regular putting drill. More than just a few spectators watched him.

VISION 54
by Dudley Peters

Five minutes before his start time, he went to the first tee. Just as he was laying down his bag, Joanie appeared from the crowd, picked up his bag, and started cleaning the clubs. Hummer smiled at her and nodded.

His foursome had two college players that were unranked amateurs, plus a ranked player, a little older than the other three, who also had qualified and played in 3 US Amateurs in recent years.

They all shook hands and got ready. Right on time, the announcer introduced the players to the crowd. Hummer was hitting second. He looked around for a moment or two, hoping to see his mom and other sister, but he didn't see them.

Everyone knew that out of the 98 players trying to qualify here, only the two lowest scores of this entire qualifying Tournament would be awarded an entry ticket to compete in the upcoming US Amateur Open.

Ninety-six of the players here would be sent home and wait for another year. Needless to say, there would be some fierce competition out there today. Each and every player held a vision that they would make it.

The USGA is the governing body of all Open Championships in the United States. The courses played are set up and approved by the USGA. For this tournament, they used the most difficult pin placements on 16 of the 18 holes. They narrowed all fairways by 10 feet. What used to be the first cut of rough, was now the second cut.

VISION 54
by Dudley Peters

The rough in the third cut was 5 inches. The first hole had two fairway bunkers on either side of the fairway. The one on the left began 265 yards out and ended 298 yards out. The right-side bunker began at 245 yards out and ended at 279 yards out.

The #1 hole was a par 4, - 445 yards in length and uphill.

Phillip Wagner had the honors and was the first to hit. He hit a very nice drive, center cut 282 yards. Then Hummer stepped up to the tee, he took a deep breath and readied himself. He closed his eyes for a moment, visualizing the shot he wanted. When he opened them, he looked at the three opponents in his foursome. He had already met them on the driving range and had shaken each of their hands.

All three had watched some of his gigantic drives on the practice range. Now, they were all waiting for him expectantly. He felt the weight of their anticipation, all wanting to see if he could, or would, crush another mammoth drive off of the tee or if he would play it safe. He felt a surge of strength in his body, and he didn't want to disappoint them.

With the crowd and his family looking on, Hummer took another deep breath, made a couple of practice swings, then stepped in, swung his driver, and connected. The ball soared **through the air, straight and true, until it landed on the** fairway some 333 yards from the tee. He quietly let out a sigh of relief to himself. The crowd applauded.

VISION 54
by Dudley Peters

As the day wore on, the difficulty of the golf course took its toll. At the end of the front nine, Hummer had scrambled for a score of two under par. Both of his playing companions were at four over. There were only a total of 7 golfers in red numbers on the big leaderboard.

As play continued, the red numbers came down to where there were now only 4 players below par, two of them at minus 2, and two of them at minus 1, also there were 6 players at even par.

One of the players that was tied with Hummer at 2 under was on his final hole of the day. He had a 16-footer for par, and he holed it. Hummer could hear the roar. The other two players that were 1 under both had bogeyed a hole, and they were now at even par, with one hole to play. Hummer was on the par 4, seventeenth hole, with a poor lie in the heavy rough just 5 yards off the green. His second shot had landed on the green, but the steep undulation caused his ball to run off and find the rough. He was about 60 feet from the hole. He muscled it onto the green some 14 feet short of the cup. When it was his turn to putt, he stroked a wonderful putt, but it didn't fall; he was now 1 under, with 1 hole to go.

Hummer knew that he needed to make a par to get in, but on the other hand, a bogey, or worse, would be a disaster. He calmly planned his strategy for the hole, then made an easy routine par. *He was in!*

Hummer rode back with a very happy Brad Davis.

# Chapter 15

When they all got back home, Joanie, Hummer, Susan, and both their parents were switching the TV to every sports channel, looking for golf news about the US Amateur Tournament. They finally found it.

They all enjoyed hearing the name Henry Muller on TV.

After dinner, Hummer was in his room getting ready to go to bed when his cell rang. It was Tommy congratulating him on qualifying. Then Joanie came in.

"You were so good today; you set yourself apart from the others, and it was noticeable. Your calmness and confidence were showing, and you came through nicely."

"Thanks, Joanie," he said. "There's still a lot of golf to be played, and I believe I'm ready. One thing I know for sure, I'm anxious."

Right then, Hummer's phone went off again. It was Tim Parlette, "Hi Hummer, this is Tim, how are you?"

"Fine, thanks."

"Congratulations on your qualifying; I'm sure the competition was excellent."

"Yes, it was; I just wish I was out of school, though."

"You know that there are ways to graduate from high school early, don't you?"

"What? No, I didn't know that. How?"

"Call your school administrator, or better yet, look it up online."

"Thanks, Tim."

"You're welcome; I'll get us some matches set up. See you later."

"Bye."

He went in and found Joanie. He asked her if she knew anything about students getting their diplomas early in their final year of High School. She said that she had heard of it but knew nothing about it. She went to the internet and searched for information. She found some. She printed it, read it, re-read it, and handed it over to Him.

Graduating high school early to start working is an option for you if you want or need to start making money right away, whether to support yourself or your family.

How to Graduate High School Early: 5-Step Guide

So, how can you graduate high school early? I've outlined the steps you need to follow below. There's a bit of math involved, but nothing you can't handle. After all, you'll soon be a high school graduate!

Step 1: Decide When You Want to Graduate

by Dudley Peters

This first step is pretty simple: all you need to do is decide how early you want to graduate high school. Do you want to graduate a semester early? An entire year? How long do you want to spend pursuing whatever it is you're doing instead of attending high school?

When figuring this out, remember that it's often easier to graduate just a semester early than a whole year. If that doesn't seem like a long enough time to you, remember that even if you only graduate a semester early, you'll finish high school in December or January. If you start college the following September, that still gives you about eight months of time to work, travel, or pursue another opportunity. **If you still need help deciding, talk to your academic advisor.** They're a great resource to have, and they'll likely be able to help make this process easier (not to mention, you'll have to let them know if you officially decide to graduate early, so you might as well start talking to them now).

Step 2: Calculate the Number of Credits You Need to Graduate

Now that you know when you want to graduate, it's time to get into the math. Almost every high school requires its students to complete a certain number of credits before they can graduate. Look in your student handbook or ask your academic advisor to find out how many credits your particular high school requires.

As an example, we'll use the high school I graduated from, which required its students to complete 21 credits, with each class worth about 0.5 credits per semester.

**First, figure out how many credits you've already completed.** You can usually find this information on your report card or transcript, or you can ask your advisor.

**Next, subtract the number of credits you've completed from the number of total credits you need to graduate.** The answer you get is the number of credits you'll need to make before you can graduate using this method. The good news for you is that the number of graduating credits for most high schools **often doesn't require you to complete four full-time years of school**. Again, for my high school, you needed to complete 21 credits to graduate, but a student attending high school full-time would complete about 7 credits each year, meaning most students at the end of their junior year would already have enough credits to graduate.

Step 3: Determine Which Classes You Need to Graduate

It's time to figure out the specific classes you need to take to graduate. Look at your student handbook or talk to your advisor to learn which classes students at your high school must take in order to graduate. This will usually require a certain number of semesters of math, English, science, and social studies, as well as some possible other requirements, such as a gym or fine arts class.

VISION 54
by Dudley Peters

Hummer liked what he read in step 2. Credits needed to graduate. He would find out the answers he needed from the school. It was possible that he already had enough. He felt good about all of this. It seemed that everything was going his way right now. Everything.

Joanie called the school and asked for an academic advisor; she got connected to Mrs. Thompson. After identifying herself, she informed the advisor about her brother, Henry, needing to be excused from his senior year.

"Does he have enough credits to make this happen, Mrs. Thompson?"

"Let me look this up for you, just a minute, please; I'm putting you on hold," Joanie waited.

A short time later, "Miss Muller; You may inform your brother that he already has enough credits to graduate. However, I recommend that he still complete his senior year in high school."

# Chapter 16

It was raining hard at the Briar Lakes Course, and the forecast called for rain for the next two days, so Hummer went home early. Dinner time wouldn't be here for 3 hours or so.

In his room, he turned the TV to mute. He closed his computer, then laid back on his bed and decided to take a quiet look at himself and what he had become, where he was, and where he was headed.

He had accomplished quite a bit with his golfing abilities in the past two and a half years. He had built up a sizeable bank account; he had managed to keep away from drugs; he split up with his girlfriend, removing that sort of anxiety and distraction. He was considering giving up beer, too; he would sometimes bring to mind some of the drinking that a few pro players got into trouble with. Mainly. Some videos in the past of John Daly and Tiger Woods and others show them in a bad light after partying and drinking. Now, he has found out he has gotten out of the burden of attending school for his senior year and still would receive his diploma and graduate. Yes, things couldn't be better.

He now had the freedom to prepare for the US Amateur Golf Tournament coming up in Colorado.

But for the most part, even with his beer drinking, he had been making money gambling on golf. This subject was something that his parents had never talked about. They would never gamble. He was certain they would never approve of his gambling. They were not told about this part of his golfing or his beer habit. These issues were kept guarded from reaching his parents.

He had players coming to him, wanting to partner up with him and gamble on golf; so far, it was working out well, very well. He couldn't quite put his finger on it, but somehow he knew it was wrong. Something there just wasn't right; he could feel it.

As for other matters pertaining to gambling on golf, they were all problematic in one way or the other; however, strange as it seems, there was a plus to be had.

The plus comes from taking a chance with your own money, risking your money, that you could outplay and beat someone in a round of golf.

This type of self-induced pressure amazingly helps sharpen and hone golfing skills, and it does it quickly. It brings about an unusual, ultra concentration toward the task at hand and strengthens the all-important mental parts of the game. Not to mention direct access to your adrenaline gland.

Hummer was feeling good right now; he felt strong, he felt like he could win regularly because of the ability and skill he had earned from all of the hard work and repetitive hours he had spent on his golf swing.

He told himself he could beat anyone, anytime. His ego woudn't let him say so out loud, however.

Hummer was fit, capable, and raring to go. He was certain nothing could go wrong; after all, he had over $15,000.00 in the bank to prove it.

After some thought as to who he should call for his next money game, Things were now different. Tommy couldn't play, so the guaranteed two grand was no longer there right now.

He decided on Tim Parlette. When he answered, Hummer said that he was thinking about a match where he could win some cash.

Tim responded, "Sure, Hummer, when would you like me to set up the match, and how much do you want your exposure to be?"

"Exposure?"

"Yes, how much money do you want to play for?"

"Oh, okay. I'd say around ten grand."

"When are you available, and where do you want to play?"

"I'd say, the sooner, the better. As to where I know every square inch at Briar Lakes, but wherever you think would be best."

"Okay, I'll get back to you as soon as I can."

"Great."

Hummer hung up; he sensed a nervous twinge in his stomach, but e dismissed it immediately. He then thought, when I pick up this 10 grand, I'll have 25 grand in the bank. He felt even better than he did before he called Tim.

Wonderful thoughts flooded through his mind, and he could have 100 grand in the bank after a few more wins. He was on cloud nine.

# Chapter 17

Hummer received a registered letter, which was delivered to his house. His mother signed for it and left it on his bed. It was from the US Amateur Open Golf Committee. USGA.

When he got home, just as darkness was setting in, his mother told him about the letter she had signed for. He raced to his bedroom, looked over the envelope closely, front and back, and then opened it. It was a single page.

The letter congratulated him for making the final 312 amateur golfers that will be competing for the title of US Amateur Champion.

The letter notified him that the Tournament would be a 7-day event held at The Cherry Hills Country Club in Cherry Hills, Colorado.

Players were to make their own living accommodations.

Practice times are available on September 9th & 10th.

All players must be registered by noon on September 9th.

Pairings will be announced on September 11th.

The Pre-tournament Banquet will be on September 11th.

The Tournament starting date is September 12th.

# VISION 54
## by Dudley Peters

The Cherry Hills Country Club is One of America's most historic golf courses. **Cherry Hills** was founded in 1922 on 272 acres just south of

Denver, and designed by renowned course architect William Flynn.

After reading the letter several times, Hummer called Brad Davis. He got no answer, so he left a message. He then called Tommy Montclair and read the letter to him. Tommy was aglow. He tells Hummer that he is going to pay the expenses for this trip. He will take care of getting all the living arrangements and whatever else is needed for the tournament.

Tommy knew that if Hummer should win, it would be a windfall for this investment and his overall plan.

Then he let Joanie read the letter, and he correctly predicted that she would want to go with him and help out in any way she could, including caddying. As far as the rest of the family, he was certain they would not plan to go to Colorado for a week.

Another thing happened. Ever since Hummer found out he already had enough credits to graduate early from high school, attending classes became a nonissue and not necessary to do, especially if he had a golf match. It was almost a utopia.

# Chapter 18

Tim Parlette called Hummer to notify him about the upcoming match.

"We have a date this coming Friday at 1:15. They want to play at Woodcrest; they're members there."

"Who are they, and what are their handicaps?" Hummer asked.

"Eddie Aviles and Glenn Stoll. They're both 6 handicappers."

"That's a lot of strokes," said Hummer. "By the way, what did you say your handicap was?"

"5, but don't worry about it. We'll win."

"How do you know?"

"As soon as they lose a hole, any hole, by missing a short putt or something similar, they lose their desire; they just give up. It's like they're destined to lose. By the way, the bet is 30 grand. You can stay at 10, or you can hold half; it's your call."

"I'd better stay at 10. Wait, on second thought, I'm in for half. Okay?"

"You got it. I'll see you Friday; get here around noon, and we can have lunch."

"Okay, bye. Wait a minute, Tim. One more thing. How does everybody pay, and when?"

"All bets are settled right after the round and in full, normally with a personal check."

"Okay, bye."

When Hummer hung up, he felt a bit strange. His stomach had a feeling of nervousness. He tried to ignore it, but the feeling persisted. He couldn't quite identify it; he only knew it was different. Whatever it was, it was bothersome and had a grip on him.

While still thinking about the big gamble he just made, he decided to ease his nerves by setting up a tune-up match. He was considering a $1,000 bet, just to ensure a win and calm his anxiety. He called his buddy, Adam Schrager.

When they talked, Adam agreed to set it up with the same two players they beat last time, except this time, they'd play at Adam's home course, Woodcrest. Hummer told Adam the match needed to be before Friday.

I'll set it up for Wednesday or Thursday. I'll call you right back," Adam said.

"Okay," Hummer replied.

Fifteen minutes later, Adam called back. "Wednesday at 10:00 am. They have to play early; Larry has to be somewhere later in the day."

"Can you pick me up again?" Hummer asked.

"Sure, 8:45 am okay?"

"I'll be ready."

Meanwhile, over at Columbia Country Club, Larry and Mike were discussing the match they had just agreed to.

"I don't know about you, but I'm tired of losing to Adam in these matches he gets us into," Larry said.

"Me too. I think we've lost 3 out of 4 so far," Mike replied.

"That's what I'm talking about. But now, with this new guy, Hummer, as a 2-man team, they're going to be hard to beat."

"You got any ideas?"

"Yeah, I'm gonna ask for a stroke adjustment. After all, we have lost 3 out of 4 matches."

"I'm with you on that."

"We need to win this time."

"Yes, we sure do."

# Chapter 19

Hummer was at the bank at 8:00 am, making sure he was the first customer. He withdrew $1,200, then headed back home to wait for Adam. Despite his best efforts to stay calm, he couldn't shake the uneasy feeling that had settled in his gut.

A short time later, Adam arrived, and they were on their way to the golf course. As they drove, Adam noticed Hummer's lack of enthusiasm and asked, "What's the matter? Is something wrong?"

"I don't know. I'll be okay, though, once we tee off."

"I hope so. I've lost some money matches since we last played. I'm counting on you to change all that."

"Don't worry, I'm ready," Hummer replied, trying to sound confident.

When they pulled up to the bag drop, the attendant grabbed their bags. Hummer changed his shoes in the car while Adam went to the men's locker room to change. They met up with their opponents, Larry and Mike, on the putting green, exchanged greetings, and started putting.

As their tee time arrived, they all stood on the first tee and agreed on a $300 Nassau bet, with $5 trash. Larry then said, "Adam, we both need one more stroke each today."

"No way," Adam replied.

"Why not? I've lost 3 out of 4 matches to you this year so far," Larry reasoned.

Hummer chimed in, "Let them each have the extra stroke. I feel good today."

"Okay, if you say so, but I'm not happy. I know these guys, you don't," Adam muttered reluctantly.

Larry tossed up a tee, and he and Mike won the honors.

The front nine proved uneventful, with Larry and Mike "ham and egging" their way to a tie. The extra stroke they had negotiated would come into play on the second hardest hole on the back nine, hole #18, with another regular stroke on hole #13.

As they started the back nine, the pattern continued, and after 13 holes, Adam and Hummer found themselves 1 down. Standing on the 14th tee, Hummer asked, "Should we take a 1 down press?"

"Yes," Adam replied.

"Okay, we press," Hummer announced.

"You got it," was the response from Larry and Mike.

They halved the next 4 holes, leading to the final hole, #18. As expected, the extra stroke came into play, and Larry and Mike secured the win with a birdie, for a net eagle. Like gentlemen, they all shook hands and exchanged pleasantries, but the loss stung.

The final tally showed that Adam and Hummer each owed $1,290.

This loss was devastating for Hummer. He did his best to hide it, but his gut was in turmoil. Getting over this defeat would take a toll on him, and it had already begun. He had been so sure of winning that it was hard to accept the reality. Worse yet, he now realized that his money was no longer safe—Hummer was in trouble.

The weight of his loss and the realization of his financial shortfall pressed heavily on him. He whispered to Adam, "I only have $1,200 with me." (Being short on a payoff in a golf bet is a major faux pas.)

Adam reassured him, "Give me the 12 hundred, and I'll pay for us both. You can pay me the 90 bucks when we get back to your house."

Hummer was now facing an even bigger problem: he didn't have enough money to cover the large bet he had committed to with Tim. The uneasy feeling that had plagued him earlier was now a full-blown crisis, hanging over him like a dark cloud.

# **Chapter 20**

Tim Parlette rings Hummer's cell. He wanted to know if the plan to meet at the course was still on, or if they would ride together.

"Yes, pick me up, please. What time should I be ready?"

"I'll be there around eleven."

"My sister wants to caddy for me, can she come along with us?"

"Sure."

"Oh, one more thing, I need to change my bet to 13 grand if that's okay with you?" Hummer asked.

"Okay, but why?"

"I had a debt to pay yesterday."

"Oh, okay."

"Are you ready for this match?"

"Sure am."

"See you tomorrow."

Hummer puts a blank check into his wallet just in case.

He now sits back and starts pondering to himself. I must be crazy. I'm jeopardizing all of the money I have saved for an entire year on a single golf match. His mind quickly jumped to, on the other hand, I could make a whole year's winnings in 4 hours tomorrow. *(typical* gamblers *thoughts.)* All of a sudden, he felt better, much better; his mojo was back, plus the stomach butterflies were gone.

Another thing came to his mind, Tommy would be able to play again soon, Hummer hoped, whenever his doctors give him the green light on his wrist. He would then be able to get back to the "2 grand/no-risk," deal he had with Tommy. This, too, made him feel better.

He called for Joanie to come to his room and then closed the door. He confided in her about what was really going on with the big bet. She listened without interrupting. When he was through, Joanie said, "Hummer, you know I am always ready to help you in any way I can?"

"Right."

"Yes."

"Well, I am totally against what you just told me. It's not the way to go. It's not the way to be proud of your accomplishments in life."

"Then why do I feel so good about it?"

"I don't know, but what I do know is that I'm right."

"You are wrong this time. You'll see," he said.

"No, I won't see. I'm not caddying if you do this."

"That's your choice, not mine."

"Well, anyway, good luck tomorrow. Tell me about it when you get home."

"Are you serious?"

Joanie doesn't answer; she leaves the room and is gone.

The next morning at 7:30, Hummer was in the kitchen, eating some cereal, when Joanie came in.

"Did you change your mind?"

"No."

"Aw, come- on."

"No way, Jose. I've got some other advice for you, too."

"What?"

"You better spend more time on the practice range than you have been doing lately."

"My game is as good as ever right now."

"It needs to be better, always better," she said.

"I do agree with that."

"Then do it."

"Okay, okay."

Tim picked up Hummer at 10:45 a.m. and asked, "Where's your caddy?"

"She decided to stay home today," Hummer replied.

VISION 54
by Dudley Peters

On the way to the golf course, Tim started up a conversation. "Listen, Hummer, we need to win today. We have to put forth everything we have to beat these guys. I want your best. You never know how the ball might bounce, you know what I mean? After all, we're talking 30 grand, don't forget that."

"Yeah, I remember. You told me these guys always find a way to lose. I already knew that was bunk."

After they left the bag drop, they went into the men's grille. They saw their opponents and went over. Tim introduced Glenn Stoll and Eddie Aviles to Hummer.

They had just finished lunch and said that they would be on the putting green. Tim ordered a grilled ham and cheese sandwich with a diet soda. Hummer said, "ditto for me."

Tee time arrived; It was a cloudy day with wind.

The bet was laid out as $ 15k on the front nine and $ 15k on the back nine, with no presses, no gimmies, and no trash. A simple stroke play match.

Tim tossed up a tee, and it pointed toward himself.

Hole #1 was a par 4, 435 yards, with a dog leg starting at about 245 yards out.

Hummer had played here only once before. "Let me go first," said Tim; "if I'm safe, you might consider going over the corner."

VISION 54
by Dudley Peters

Tim hit a horrible duck-hook shot that flew into the woods about 220 yards from the tee. Hummer asked, "How far is it to the woods straight out from here?"

"About 345 yards," came the reply.

"Okay, thanks." Hummer then hit his three-wood about 40 yards short of the woods. It was in good shape.

Both Glenn and Eddie hit nice drives out past the dogleg corner, setting themselves up with nice shots into the green. Tim found his ball and chipped it out onto the fairway. All three were getting a stroke here. Tim hit again, with his ball stopping ten yards short of the green. Eddie hit his six-iron onto the green about 30 feet away. Hummer was next, cutting his seven-iron onto the green seven feet from the hole.

Glenn then hit his seven-iron onto the green, leaving himself an 18-footer. Tim chipped up, his ball didn't go in, so he asked Eddie to hit it back to him. Eddie lined up his birdie putt, took the shot, and missed. Tim hit it back to him, conceding the par. Glenn lined up his putt and took the shot, but left it one inch short. It was kicked back. Hummer looked over his seven-footer from both sides, took longer than usual to set up, and then putt it into the center of the cup for the birdie and the halve.

Hole #2: They halved the second hole as well.

Hole #3: On the third hole, a par 3, no one received a stroke. Tim sank a nice birdie putt, putting Hummer and Tim one-up.

Hole #4: This was a 537-yard, very long par five. All three were getting a stroke. All the players were on in three, except for Hummer. He had a 45-foot putt for eagle and would be putting first. Hummer sized everything up and stroked the putt. It missed to the left and stopped 18 inches from the hole. Eddie hit it back to him, so Hummer was in with a birdie. Next was Glenn, who had a longish putt that was uphill with just a little right-to-left bend, a desirable putt for most right-handers. Glenn readied himself, putt, and drained it for birdie, net eagle. It was now up to Tim to tie the hole. Tim got the dreaded lip-out, and the match went back to even heading to the fifth tee.

Holes #5 and #6: Both of these holes were halved with routine pars.

Hole #7: Eddie and Glenn were the only players to get a stroke on this hole. Both Hummer and Tim knew that one of them would more than likely make par for a net birdie. So, they also knew that one of themselves needed to birdie the hole just for a halve.

Tim's ball was in the fairway, 150 yards away, but sitting in a very deep divot that someone had not repaired. It was as ugly as it could be. He swung his seven-iron, hoping to dig it out. The ball did come out and made it all the way to the upslope, nine yards short of the putting surface. Hummer was left with one of his favorite shots—a nine-iron with a nice lie, and perfect distance for him. He stroked it, and it went extremely high. When it came down, it hit the edge of a sprinkler head and bounded off into the woods. He went over to it but found he had no straight shot at the pin from where he was. Glenn and Eddie both made par and took a one-up lead, with two holes remaining on the front side.

Tim could see that Hummer was upset with what had happened and tried to console him.

"I knew something like this was going to happen; I could feel it," said Hummer.

Tim decided to leave him alone since he was clearly hot.

Hole #8 was the other par 5 on this nine. This hole was halved when Eddie sank a difficult, slick 15-footer.

Hole #9: They reached the tee. This hole was a par 4, 396 yards straight away with a lake in front of the green. Hummer treated this hole as a "must-win" in his mind.

Glenn boomed one out into the center of the fairway, followed by Eddie with a nice drive as well, landing on the edge of the fairway. Tim then hit a nice drive into the fairway, too. Hummer brought out his driver.

"How far to the lake?" he asked.

"Don't worry about it, it's 375 yards," came the reply.

Hummer teed up his ball, took several practice swings, stepped up, lined himself up, and then connected. It was a mammoth drive— very high and very long, right down the middle. All three of the guys looked at each other in awe.

VISION 54
by Dudley Peters

"That was the longest and highest drive I have ever seen," said Tim.

"You said it. Me too. Wow."

Hummer's ball had stopped just 5 yards in front of the lake; he was only 21 yards from the hole.

Eddie hit first, getting on with a nice six-iron shot, just a bit long. Tim put his ball in the middle of the green, with only 20 feet left. Glenn hit his seven-iron, making a wonderful shot that wound up a mere 15 inches from the hole.

No one was getting any strokes, so Hummer knew he had to make his chip shot to win the hole and halve the front nine. A tie here wouldn't help. He hit a beautiful shot that stopped just 4 inches short of the hole.

Glenn hit it back to him. Tim and Hummer couldn't concede Glenn's putt with so much on the line. They could only watch as he stroked it into the center of the cup.

They pulled up to the clubhouse. Tim asked what everyone wanted to drink or eat. They responded with their orders, and then Hummer said, "I'll have a Miller Lite and a pack of orange crackers, thanks."

The girl came out and delivered the order to them. Hummer snapped open the tab and guzzled down a third of the beer with his first swig. Tim noticed and made a mental note for future reference.

"Hey, Hummer, I didn't know you were a beer drinker," Tim said.

"Yeah, sometimes I play a lot better after a few beers. I'm hoping today will be one of those," Hummer replied.

"Me too, but I, personally, never drink during an important golf match. Get my drift?" said Tim.

"Yeah, but we should have never lost that front nine. Hitting that sprinkler head killed us," said Hummer.

"Well, anyway, we need to win the back nine and get out of the trap. I don't believe that beer is what will do it for us," Tim said.

"We'll see," Hummer answered.

The tee was open. Tim said to Hummer, "Well, at least I'll be getting three shots on this nine and take back that advantage they talked us into on the front."

# Chapter 21

## <u>BACK NINE BEGINS</u>

#10 was a par 5, 535 yards long. All 3 got a stroke here, again.

When they had all reached the green, Hummer had an eagle putt to win the hole, but he missed it, and the hole was halved.

#11 was a fairly short par 4, dogleg. There were 3 balls in the fairway, all of them just a 7 or 8 iron away. No one was getting a stroke.

Hummer asked Tim what he thought about him trying to cut the corner and drive the green.

"You have got to hit it pretty high to clear those tall trees, and the carry must be at least 310 yards," Tim said.

"I'm going for it," Hummer replied. He hit the driver, high and long, and it sailed above the trees, cutting the dogleg. His ball bounced up onto the green 28 feet from the pin.

"Nice shot," they all said.

Tim was to hit his approach shot first. He selected his 7-iron, hit it hard, and got it on the green just 19 feet from the hole. Hummer clapped after the shot. Eddie was next. He hit his 8-iron; it came up just a little short but was puttable from off the green. It was about 25 feet. Glenn pondered for a moment, either a hard 9 or a medium 8-iron. He decided on a hard 9. He stroked it nicely; it hit the green, grabbed on, and stopped abruptly, just 13 feet from the hole. Eddie clapped. They all walked up to the green with putters in hand.

The cart girl pulled up and waited.

While on the green, Hummer, once more, just barely missed the eagle but was ceded the birdie. It was good enough to win the hole and go 1-up on the back nine. He went straight over to the cart girl, got 2 beers, opened one, and put one in the mini-cooler on the cart that was already full of ice. Nobody else got anything.

#12 was a par 3, 180 yards to an elevated green, and well-bunkered. No one was getting a stroke here. Tim hit a choked-down 5-iron, and it barely stayed on the green. It was a long way from the hole. Hummer selected his 7-iron and put it 18 feet from the pin. Eddie hit his 5-iron, hooked it badly left, hit an oak tree, careened off, and ended up 8 feet from the hole. Glenn also chose a 5-iron, choked down on it, and hit a nice shot to the middle of the green.

Tim was the first to putt. He hit a poor putt, left it 10 feet short, elected to continue, and missed again. He reached down, picked up his ball, and put it in his pocket. No one said anything. It was now Glenn's turn. He conferred with Eddie, lined it up, then stroked it. He left it 1 inch short and made par. It was now Hummer's turn to putt. He asked Tim about the break. He then readied himself and putt; again, he just barely missed the eagle but was ceded a birdie. It was now Eddie's turn. He needed this 8-footer to halve the hole. He lined it up, stroked it, and it hit the edge of the hole and stayed out—another par. Tim and Hummer were now 2-up on the back nine.

Hole #13 was a long par 4, 439 yards, uphill. All 3 got a stroke here. Tim got off a nice drive into the fairway. Hummer hit a mammoth drive, missed the fairway, but had a decent lie in the rough. Eddie got a nice drive into the fairway, and so did Glenn.

Tim was away, 189 yards to the hole, got out his rescue club, and hit it. It hit just short of the green, rolled to the left, and hopped into the bunker. Glenn had 180 yards. He selected his 5-iron and hit a nice shot to the frog hair some 25 feet from the hole. Eddie also hit the 5-iron onto the green. He was 28 feet away. Hummer looked over his lie; he had 136 yards left to the hole. He brought out the 9-iron and cut it into 10 feet. Tim hit his sand iron. The ball did a one-hop-stop, a foot from the hole. Hummer clapped. It was Eddie's turn; he lined up his putt and, with perfect speed, made the birdie. It won the hole. Tim and Hummer were now 1-up on the back.

Hole #14 was a 398-yard par 4. Four fairway bunkers and water came into play; up by the green, there was a lake there. There were no handicap strokes here. Eddie hit a decent drive into the fairway, 255 yards out. Glenn muscled another nice drive into the first cut of rough, some 265 yards out. Tim sliced one out of their 250 yards that caught a bunker. Then Hummer hit a pure shot 300 yards.

Tim hit a 7-wood out of the bunker, and it landed in the fairway 15 yards short of the green. Eddie selected his 8-iron and hit it onto the green some 30 feet away. Glenn then hit his 9-iron, and it wound up right next to Eddie's ball. Hummer got out his 58° lob wedge, then hit his ball onto the green; it stopped 6 inches from the hole, and Tim clapped as he picked up his ball.

Glenn decided to go first, and they talked about the putt. Eddie positioned himself directly behind Glenn. The line for Glenn's putt, looked to be about a 16-inch break. He looked at it for a long time, then he putt, and his ball came to rest just past the hole on the high side. He picked it up. Eddie moved his temporary ball marker back into the correct position, placed his ball down, and then picked up the marker. He knew exactly what the putt was going to do. He lined himself up, got in good posture, and then putt. The ball went into the center of the cup for the halve, and Eddie and Glenn high-fived it all the way off the green. But they remained 1-down on the back, with 4 holes to go.

Hole #15 was a 175-yard par 3. No strokes on this hole. All 4 players made par. Eddie and Glenn remained 1-down, now with 3 holes to go.

Hole #16 was a par 4, 405 yards. No strokes on this hole, either. All 4 players were in the fairway. Eddie was away; he had 150 yards left, selected a 7-iron, and made a nice swing. The ball went a little long to the back portion of the green. Tim was next. He grabbed his 8-iron and hit a decent shot to about 18 feet. Glenn was just 130 yards from the hole. He selected his pitching wedge. He hit it a little thin, it scooted past the hole, and stopped 25 feet away. Hummer got out his lob wedge again, made a nice swing, and popped it up high into the air; it came down just 5 feet from the hole.

Eddie, Glenn, and Tim all two-putted for par. Hummer needed to make this easy 5-footer. He missed. He started to get really disgusted with himself; he knew he had it. He knew that he could never miss such an easy putt. Even after the calamity, they were still 1-up with 2 to go.

Hole #17 was a par 4, 430 yards, dogleg left. The final stroke hole for all 3 players. Eddie drove one just past the dogleg opening, in good shape. Glenn also hit a nice drive about ten yards past Eddie. Tim teed it up high and hit his best drive of the day, a beauty that made its way around the dogleg and into the fairway.

Hummer asked Tim if he should try to go over the trees and cut the dogleg.

"Why don't you just take it around the corner like I did?" Tim replied.

"Okay, but not with my driver; I must use my 3-wood for that shot," Hummer said.

"Sounds good to me."

"Okay."

Hummer got out his 3-wood, took a few practice strokes, stepped up, and connected. His ball started hooking way too early and landed in the woods with no shot to the green. He chipped his ball out and got back into play. He was still away, with 232 yards to the hole. They decided that Tim should go first. This way, it would make it a much easier decision about Hummer's next shot.

Tim had 181 yards to the middle of the green. He got out the 4-iron and caught a flyer; it landed on the back of the green some 50 feet from the hole. Hummer now had to go for it. He took several practice swings with his rescue club, lined himself up, and hit a magnificent golf shot with a little fade. The ball hit the green, rolled up, and stopped 4 feet from the hole. Tim clapped and said, "Nice shot."

Glenn was next; he had 190 yards to the pin. He selected his 7-wood and hit a good shot to about 20 feet. Eddie gave him a high-five. Now it was Eddie's turn; he had 179 yards to the pin. He had a 6-iron in his hand. He made a nice stroke. The ball got on the green, leaving him with a flat 19-footer for birdie.

Tim asked Hummer for his read on his putt. Hummer said it looked like a double breaker. He walked about halfway and pointed with his putter to the spot he thought Tim needed to aim for. Hummer then said,

"It's a little downhill, so don't kill it."

Tim took his time, lined it up, got into a good position, and struck it. It went toward the hole but stopped woefully short, leaving him with an 11-footer for par. Both Eddie and Glenn made two-putt pars. Hummer picked up his ball already lying 3. Tim had to make this putt. He missed to the left. The back nine was now even going into #18.

Hummer, now quite upset with himself, stormed off to the cart, grabbed his last beer, snapped open the tab, and guzzled almost half with the first swallow. Tim said nothing. He could easily tell that nothing he could say would calm him down or help.

Hole #18 was a par 5, 495 yards, straightaway hole with 3 fairway bunkers and a lake in front that wrapped around the left side of the green. The lake was definitely a disaster if you got in it. The only good news was that the hole was a par 5, and there were no strokes coming to anyone.

Eddie hit a nice drive to the edge of the fairway. Glenn sliced his drive into the rough. Tim hit another beautiful drive into the fairway. Hummer, being a little upset, teed his ball high. He connected with his driver. It was a mammoth drive right down the middle; there was no doubt he would be on in two.

Eddie was away and first to hit; he was at the 245-yard marker. He laid up to around 80 to 90 yards. He swung his 7-iron, and his ball stopped at the 95-yard marker. Tim was next; he, too, laid up with a 7-iron, leaving him 88 yards. Glenn hit the 8-iron, and it stopped at the 70-yard marker.

Hummer was between clubs. He had 204 yards left to the hole. The shot was going to be either a soft 5-iron or a hard 6-iron. He settled on the hard 6. He had a decent lie. He lined himself up and made a hard swing; the ball went to the left and landed in the lake. He slammed the club down to the ground, not once, but several times. He was livid.

Eddie was away; he hit his wedge onto the green and left himself with a 16-footer. Next was Tim; he hit his wedge onto the green to about 17 feet. Next was Glenn; he hit his sand iron, and the ball stopped just 11 feet from the hole.

Hummer took a drop in front of the lake and hit the lob wedge to about 5 feet. Tim was to putt first; he didn't ask Hummer for any help. His putt skirted the hole, and the par was conceded. Eddie was next to putt; he lined it up and left it 2 inches short. It, too, was conceded. Then Glenn lined up his putt and dropped in the birdie for the win. They all shook hands as a routine, but Hummer couldn't get out of there quickly enough. He pulled out the check, made it out to cash for $13,000.00, handed it to Tim, and then said he had to go.

"Okay, Hummer, I'll go get the car."

"Not necessary; my buddy is on his way to get me. I texted him, he'll be right here."

"Whatever you say. Call me later, okay?"

No answer.

Hummer was sick; he felt like he was going to throw up, his mind was developing a headache, and he was starting to get the shakes. Everything was bothering him all at once. He couldn't wait to get home and go to bed. His buddy Mark picked him up; he threw the clubs and shoes in the trunk, got in, and slammed the door.

"Are you okay, man?"

"Do I look okay?"

"No, but don't take it out on me."

"I'll take it out on anybody I want."

"Look, man, I'm taking you home; I'm not saying anything else."

"Good."

# Chapter 22

Hummer got home and went right to his room. He laid back on his bed with all of his clothes on. His mind was racing. He was truly ill. He had never felt this bad, not even close. His mind told him to quit golf. He developed a fever. His mind told him that he was a total failure, a loathsome hypocrite. He had betrayed his family and would lose their love and respect. He believed they would repudiate him and make him move out. He thought of himself as a greedy liar, especially towards his family. How stupid and unworthy was his decision to gamble every dollar he had saved? Why was money driving his being?

Now, Hummer's mental system started coming down with MDD - (Major Depressive Disorder). He felt like he didn't want to go on. He lay there on the bed, then got into the fetal position. He was in a world of hurt. The sun was beginning to set. The room went semi-dark, but he didn't care; he never moved. Joanie came home and knocked on his bedroom door. There was no answer. She entered, flipped on the light, went over, and asked:

"What's the matter?" No answer.

She noticed him shivering; she felt his head. It was hot, very hot.

"Hummer, what's going on? You have a fever and the shakes." Again, no answer.

"I'll get you some cold water and make you some chicken soup." Still no answer. She came back into the room with a tray.

"Hummer, here, take a drink of water and eat this soup."

"Leave me alone, I don't want anything."

"What happened?"

"I'm a total disgrace. I've ruined everything. I'm a greedy hypocrite and a total loser. My family will never respect or trust me ever again once they find out what I have done and what I am." He began to cry.

All of a sudden, he had a convulsion. He threw up and rolled into a knot. Joanie called 911. He wouldn't let her come near him. He hollered and screamed; it was like he was out of his mind.

The ambulance got there, he was sedated, and then they took him to the emergency room at the hospital. Joanie rode with him. An hour and a half later, he woke up. "Where am I?" he asked.

"In the hospital. You had a violent convulsion at home. You were semi-conscious. I called 911," said Joanie.

"How long have I been here?"

"Going on two hours now. I think they pumped your stomach and gave you a couple of cc's of medicine with a syringe."

"Oh Joanie, I'm in so much trouble with my life; I'm never going to recover."

"Just because you lost all of your money?" she asked. "You did lose, didn't you?"

"Yes, and also, I quit golf."

"You listen to me, Hummer; I am going to get you back on track. I'm going to fix whatever you broke. You can count on it. It's going to take some doing, but I know it can be done. You must get yourself well first, then I'm taking over."

"Where are Mom and Dad?"

"They had to go to a retirement party for one of Dad's friends at work. Mom left to go meet him earlier."

"I don't know, Joanie, I made a huge mistake, really huge."

"You can tell me about it later. Right now, I need to find out when you can go home. I'll be right back."

Joanie came back with a young doctor. He gave some instructions to Hummer and handed Joanie a prescription. They were back home 30 minutes later. Hummer was in a deep sleep five minutes after he got into his bed.

Joanie took a shower, put on her robe, and then looked in on Hummer. She quietly closed his door, went to her room, and laid back on her bed. She began to form a plan for how to bring her brother back to his normal self. She correctly figured that in his current mental state, he could easily go into a deep depression. His full recovery would be her immediate goal; she would nurse him back into good mental health and recapture the wonderful personality he once possessed. His love of golf, she thought, should not be too difficult to rekindle. His abilities on a golf course would be the least of the problems she would take on. This would be the goal and task at hand. She also knew that any gambling of any kind would be forbidden.

She knew that she would be required to put her personal life on hold. For how long? She didn't know, but she would do it. She loved her brother for the way he once was, and she was determined to get him back. The return path would begin tomorrow. She was fully committed.

# **Chapter 23**

The following morning, at 8:30 AM, Joanie called Mrs. Thompson at Bethesda High School. She asked how she could go about getting Hummer's diploma. Mrs. Thompson replied, "I remember talking to you about your brother graduating early."

"Yes, that was me. Thank you again for your help."

"Oh, you are most welcome."

Joanie was told she could pick it up in person, or they could mail it. The school, however, would prefer that it be handed out at the June graduation ceremony.

"Thank you, thank you very much, but I will need to pick it up this morning. Unless there's a problem."

"Oh no, there is no problem; I will have it ready for you."

"Thank you again, Mrs. Thompson."

Hummer knew nothing about anything Joanie was doing or planning. He was down in the dumps, in a bad way. He was lying in his bed thinking only bad thoughts when Joanie came in. "How are you, Hummer?" she asked.

"Horrible, I can't even think straight."

"I have something for you to see," he said nothing. She handed him the manila envelope.

"What's this?" she didn't answer.

by Dudley Peters

He opened it and saw the diploma. It affected him; he perked up noticeably. Joanie was careful and kept quiet. A couple of minutes later, he laid it on the bedside table and withdrew somewhat. She grasped the moment quickly and said,

"Hummer, you did it, you graduated. This is a great achievement. We all want you to succeed, and you did."

In Joanie's mind, it was a very good start for the task ahead.

"Come on, Hummer, I want you to go somewhere with me and my friend Clara. Get ready, she'll be here in 15 minutes."

He put on his pants and golf shirt, then picked up the diploma again and read it.

"Here she is, come on."

Clara drove them to the Burger King drive-thru window, and they ordered. Country music was playing on the radio. The mood in the car was fairly good. They pulled into a nearby park, found a nice spot, parked, and ate. The music and songs couldn't have been more perfect. Hummer was having a good time. Joanie knew for sure that this beginning was going nicely, especially when Hummer aimed and blew his straw wrapper like a blowgun at her. The next thing that happened was not so good. Hummer stopped having a good time; he asked to go home. Joanie knew that now was not the time to talk him out of it. They went home. Joanie thanked Clara, and then she went into the house with Hummer.

He went to his bedroom and laid back on the bed. His system was uneasy; he felt nervous and confused. He had only bad thoughts.

Again, he told himself he was an unworthy, disgusting person. He hated himself.

Joanie was observing and trying to plan the best way to overcome some of these problems. She decided to bring golf back into the picture.

She already knew that golf had been the love of his life. He had always loved it since he was very young. It had taken over his entire life. He was self-taught, and he had qualified for the U.S. Amateur Championship.

Yes, this would be the next step on the hard road back. She began to strategize.

# Chapter 24

### <u>The hard road back</u>

It was now the middle of March; Spring golf had already started. Hummer's mind couldn't have been any further away regarding golf. He meant it when he said he quit golf.

His mind told him all of his troubles came directly from golf. He was definitely through.

The next morning, Joanie brought Hummer a plate of sausage and eggs that she had fixed. It hit the spot.

"Thank you, Joanie, that was good."

"You're welcome. Do you remember me telling you I was going to take over and fix whatever you broke?"

"Yes, I remember."

"Well, I put my own life on hold to do just that. Have you ever noticed?"

"Geeze."

"Listen, Just a short while ago, you were Humpy Dumpty, and I'm the one putting you back together, so don't make it harder than it needs to be, get it?"

"Okay, sure. Yes, I get it."

"Now, listen up, you must pledge to me, your little sister, that you will help me, and yourself, with the things I'm going to ask of you. Okay?"

"Okay, Joanie. I never even thought anything about what you have been doing and going through for me. Boy, I am so sorry."

"I'm going to ask some things of you that you might not like, but you must somehow bring yourself to do them. Okay?"

"Whatever you say, Boss."

"Tomorrow morning, we are going to the driving range."

"What?"

"You promised," Joanie said.

"What time?"

"Nine thirty."

Without mentioning anything to Hummer, Joanie goes into her room and calls Brad Davis, the Pro at Briar Lakes. He answers. She identifies herself and asks for a private meeting with just the two of them.

"Of course, Joanie, when?"

"As soon as possible."

"I'm free today at one o'clock. I'll be here in my office."

"I'll be there, and thank you."

by Dudley Peters

She walked into the pro shop just before one o'clock. Brad invites her back into his office.

"What can I help you with, Joanie?"

She related every detail about Hummer being taken to the hospital, his breakdown, and a near mental stroke. She also mentioned about him quitting golf. She left nothing out. Brad listened and was tuned in to everything. He was deeply concerned and said so.

Joanie said that she planned to get in touch with Tommy, Tim, and Adam regarding the gambling. She asked Brad if he could help with this part of the problem. He said he absolutely would.

Joanie then told Brad about the current situation and how she had partly brought him back.

She told Brad about this morning and how she got him to pledge to her that he would get back to practicing.

"Did he say when he might start?"

"Yes, we both will be here tomorrow morning at 9:30."

"Joanie, you are a wonderful Sister to Hummer, not to mention a valuable asset."

"Well, thank you for saying that."

"I'll get with those three golfers you mentioned and get back to you. I'm certain they will all support you and Hummer all the way."

She left and went back home. So far, the recovery plan appeared to be on track.

Brad sent a text to all three that he wanted to meet with them on Thursday at 1 o'clock at his office. The meeting was regarding Hummer. Important. If anyone can't make it, call me.

At the meeting, Brad related everything, especially that Joanie was in charge.

After their meeting, Brad texted Joanie to call him. She did immediately. Over the phone, he told her that all three were in total agreement. They would be supporters 100%.

She thanked him and hung up. She would relay this news to Hummer at the appropriate time.

A short time later, Tommy phoned Joanie and asked if he could meet with the two of them ASAP. She said sure, just let me know when.

They agreed. Tomorrow, at the course around lunchtime, he would treat. She said okay, we'll see you there, and thank you.

The next day, Tommy made it very clear to them that all of his commitments were still in effect. You needn't worry. If there's anything you need from me, just call. I'm with you all the way.

Hummer said, "Thanks, Tommy."

Joanie also thanked him. When lunch was over, Tommy left.

Preparing for the US Amateur continues.

At one-thirty, they both headed back out to the range; Hummer started hitting balls.

He had not actually lost any of his abilities. After all, it was just one round of golf that had caused this devastation, and that was just a few days ago.

Over the next few weeks, along with his new program, he started playing with his buddy Mark again. It was like when he was just learning about the game of golf that he dearly loved. Hummer was starting to become his old self. He was getting rejuvenated.

Later that day, at home, Hummer went into his room, closed the door and laid back once more. Looked at the ceiling and reassessed himself. This time, it wasn't self-destruction.

It was more like building confidence in himself as well as feeling good about getting better at golf. The thing he loved to do. ~~on~~ his 18th birthday was coming up, and he gave a few moments to think about that.   A few seconds later, he was asleep.

# Chapter 25

## <u>US Amateur Information</u>

Across the nation, over 8,000 amateur golfers, all over the United States and in other countries, sign up to earn a playing slot in the US Amateur. After one day of qualifying at selected golf courses all across the country, out of the 8,000, there will be just 312 players that move on. Then, after 2 days of *stroke play*, the field will be reduced to 64 players.

Then, a knockout competition is held at *match play* to decide the champion. All knockout matches are over 18 holes except for the final, which consists of 36 holes, separated into morning and afternoon 18-hole rounds. Nowadays, it is usually won by players in their late teens or early twenties who are working towards a career as a *tournament professional*.

Hummer was one of 312 amateurs that had made it this far. With the number being such a big number, many a standby would be called to fill in. That was normal.

All 312 players were mailed a complete list of all qualified players, with pertinent information on each one.

When Hummer got his package, he seated himself in the big recliner in the TV room and started reading the names.

There were so many, he didn't even read all of them, but so far, he knew no one.

He kept scanning through the names and other information. He noticed a player who lived in the Rockville area, just across the Potomac River, in Virginia. His name was Dave Hetherington.

He was a young player on the golf team at Florida Atlantic University; he was 19 years old.

Hummer kept reading names; there were players, players, and more players. It dawned on him. It would take quite some doing to survive with these many competitors.

He laid the papers down. Leaned back and started thinking, it will probably be some lucky shot or a freak bounce that will eventually produce the Champion.

Hummer wanted to win the US Amateur title badly, really bad. He knew that practicing and honing his game would need to be done right up to the time of tee-off.

A couple of days later, Hummer had a thought that he would try to phone Dave Hetherington and introduce himself. He googled his name; there were only three Hetherington's displayed. He would call all three if necessary. He got lucky; the moment he mentioned the US Amateur, he was given Dave's cell number.

He dialed it, Dave answered. Hummer introduced himself.

"Yes, I saw your name too. Rockville, right?"

"Yes, that's me. Have you got a minute?"

"Well, I'm playing right now; it has to be short."

"I just figured we could pal up at Cherry Hills, you know what I mean?"

"Let's do it. I have your number. I'll call later; I'm up."

No call was made by David or Hummer. Their meeting-up would have to wait.

There were now only 5 weeks 'til the US Amateur began. Between now and the day they would leave, at practice, Hummer would hit around 800 golf shots a day, every day, including rainy or any other type of bad weather day. He would be ready, for sure. His game would be razor-sharp and honed.

The day arrived, Joanie was the only other family member who was going to Colorado. They landed and hired an Uber to get to the hotel. Tommy met them in the lobby. He had already checked them both in. He handed them their room keys.

"Why don't you both go and unpack, freshen up, and meet me here in the lobby in, say, about an hour."

"Sounds good," said Hummer.

"Then we could ride over to Cherry Hills and walk around and look at the course and everything."

Joanie and Hummer totally agreed. Hummer's phone went off. It was Dave Hetherington.

"Hey Hummer, where are you staying?"

"The Hyatt."

"I'm at the Red Roof Inn."

"By yourself?"

"No, both of my brothers and my Dad are here."

"Well, good luck tomorrow; I'll try to find you in the morning."

"I got Monday's pairing sheet. All strangers. We only need to be in the top 64 after two rounds."

"Yeah, I know. We only have to beat a mere 248 of them."

"Hey David, have you ever played here before?"

"Yeah. My college team had a match here last year."

"Anything I should look out for?"

"Yes, the course was fast, and the greens were really fast."

"See you tomorrow."

# Chapter 26

<u>US Amateur Golf Tournament</u>

Joanie and Hummer rode with Tommy. They grabbed a quick fast food breakfast sandwich on the way; when they got there, Hummer was surprised and happy to learn Brad Davis, Tim, and Adam were there for support, too.

The weather was gorgeous, but there was a wind factor. They got there early; Hummer walked around looking for David. He saw a Team bag that said Florida Atlantic Owls. He looked around, and then this guy came over and asked, "You wouldn't be Hummer, would you?"

"David?"

"That would be me. Nice to meet you; what say, after we play, do you think we could all go to an early dinner?"

"Sounds good, but I can't answer right now. I don't know what my people have in mind."

"Where do you play back home?"

"Briar Lakes."

"I played there once. A few years ago. Well, anyway, let me know about tonight, just text me. Good luck today."

"You too."

by Dudley Peters

The first foursome teed off; it would be an hour before Hummer started. He began his practice routine. He found a spot on the driving range and started; surprisingly, there was only a small crowd of observers. He cleared his mind and got started. Joanie asked how he was feeling. Great was the answer.

He got himself well loosened up. Then they went to the practice bunker. He hit a series of sand shots. He then moved to the chipping green and hit another series of short chips. Joanie grabbed his bag, and they went to the putting green. He stayed there longer than normal, putting from everywhere. Joanie informed him, "We're up in 5 minutes."

He went over and met the other three players; their mood was quiet and surreal.

An official offered each player the chance to choose a small, folded card. They opened them; Hummer was hitting second.

Because today and tomorrow's play were both stroke play, Brad told Hummer 148, or anything below that would get him under the cut line. He felt certain of this. Hummer thought to himself, I'm going for 144 or better.

At the end of the round, Hummer had carded a 71; he was low round in his foursome. After all the scores were posted, there were 9 players who had better scores than him. Surprisingly, David Hetherington was one of those. He had carded a 70. The low round of the day was 67; 3 golfers shared that score.

by Dudley Peters

Hummer's phone dinged. It was David.

"Hey Buddy, nice round. I see that I nipped you."

"You sure did; grats to you."

"Hummer, we can't dine together tonight; my father has got us all doing something else."

"Don't worry about it. Good luck tomorrow."

"You too, I'll text you later."

They decided to go to Carrabba's Italian restaurant. Table of 6. It was perfect. Tommy paid the entire tab.

When Hummer got back to his room, Joanie came in; they talked for a few minutes, and she was making sure that nothing was hurting or bothering him. His phone dinged. It was a text from Brad; he wanted to tell him about two situations coming up tomorrow. He asked Hummer to call when he could. He called immediately.

"I was just now lying on my bed, and there are two things I want to pass on to you."

"Okay."

"On hole 8, make certain you stay left with the drive, and on 11, whatever you do, do not go long; it's bogey for sure from back, behind the green. Okay?"

"Thanks, see you tomorrow."

The next morning, just before the start, David came over, said hi to Joanie, and then said good luck to Hummer.

Hummer said, "I'm going off early today. I saw where you went late."

"Yeah, 11:50. You want to make a side bet?"

"I don't think so, but ask Joanie."

"Well, Joanie, how 'bout it, do we have a bet?"

"No, thank you. We don't gamble."

Hummer's tee time was 10 minutes away. They prepared to head on over.

When tee time arrived, they shook hands with each other and drew a card. Hummer was hitting first.

There was a sizeable crowd there; Hummer teed the ball up high, took a few practice swings, stepped in, and connected. The sound of the percussion snapped a few heads around. It was another very high and very long drive, center cut. It stopped some 344 yards from the tee. It brought a lot of applause. One of the observers was David Hetherington.

Hummer posted a round of 69 for a 140 total. Tommy, Brad, Tim, Adam, and Joanie were very happy and confident.

Later in the day, David posted another 70; he, too, was in with 140.

by Dudley Peters

Both Hummer and David had made the 64 finalists.

Tomorrow, the Knockout competition would start using Match Play.

The pairing sheet would be available right after all of today's matches were completed. You could either download it from the website or pick it up in person on-site.

There was a rumor floating around saying that only 5 players of the 64 were over 30 years old; the rest were in their twenties or late teens.

Back at the hotel, Joanie came running in with tomorrow's pairing sheet.

Hummer was playing against a golfer from Myrtle Beach, Dick Sevila. They were placed in the afternoon group. The tee time was 12:48 PM.

Joanie got out the fact sheet she had brought with her from home. They read everything about Dick Sevila that was on the sheet. Nothing stood out except he was 33 years old.

Out of curiosity, Hummer looked up at David. He was in the morning group, playing against a golfer from San Diego, Louis Bayhylle. Their tee time was 7:48 AM.

Note: After today's play, the 64 players would become 32 and then 16. Then, in tomorrow's play, the 16 players would become 8, then 4, and then 2. These two players would then play two 18-hole matches, with one of them becoming the U.S. Amateur Champion. He would receive the Havemeyer Trophy and the Gold Medal.

When Hummer's match with Dick Sevila got started, Sevila was having trouble with his drives; he was hooking every one of them, some with horrible duck hooks. Hummer had such a big lead at the turn the match ended after the 11th hole, 8 and 7.

The afternoon matches started at 2:00 PM. Hummer was paired with another college team player from Texas, Eduardo Aviles; he was 21 years old and played for UTEP (University of Texas, El Paso).

This match proved to be an extremely tough one; Aviles was very long off the tee, too. They each had 3 birdies on the first nine holes. The match was even. The back nine was exciting to watch. The back nine was nip and tuck. Hummer made a long birdie on the 18th hole for the win. Eduardo shook hands and congratulated Hummer as gentlemen do.

There were now only 16 players still alive to win the title.

Joanie waited around the clubhouse until the pairing sheet came out; she grabbed one and took off. She found Hummer and handed it to him. He was playing against a 20-year-old that was a member of Stanford's golf team. His name was Glenn Swain. Tee Time was set at 7:58 AM.

There would be three "knockout rounds" played tomorrow.

VISION 54
by Dudley Peters

Later, at the hotel, Joanie suggested they stay in. She would go get something, and they could eat in the room. Hummer said, "Okay, but we better ask Brad and them."

"Okay, but I'll be waking you up pretty early in the morning; plus, you must plan to play possibly 3 matches. Rest will come in handy tonight."

"You're right; I'll call them now."

They were receptive and understood. "See you tomorrow," Tommy said.

The next morning, the weather was fair, with the sun rising. Hummer shook hands with Glenn.

Once more, Hummer drew the honors; they both played good golf, but Hummer managed to win the front, one-up.

On the back nine, they halved 10 and 11. On the par 3, 12th, Glenn, with a nice birdie, evened the match.

When they reached the long par 5, hole #15, Hummer went 1-up again with a birdie. Hummer also won #16 and became dormy in the match. When they halved #17, Hummer advanced.

The field was now just 8 players (2 foursomes).

Pairings and tee times were upcoming. With everyone standing at the big scoreboard, the official posted the pairings. Hummer would be going second, playing against Mark Hogan from North Carolina University.

## VISION 54
### by Dudley Peters

On the first tee, Hummer drew a card; he would be hitting second. This match also was a hard-fought one, with lead changes every 3 holes. Hummer finally won 2 holes in a row on the back nine, which got him the win.

The field was now down to 4 players, one of which was David Hetherington.

Everybody gathered around the big scoreboard once more, waiting to see who played whom. Finally, it was posted: Hummer was playing Ron Devine, who was a member of the James Madison University golf team.

They met on the tee, exchanged pleasantries, and then drew a card; Hummer was hitting second. It was another grueling round; both players were determined to win. At the turn, the match was even. The back nine was nip and tuck.

Going into hole #17, the match was even. Devine hit his approach shot, got a bad bounce, and wound up under the lip of the greenside bunker. He had no choice but to go out sideways. Hummer won the hole with par. One up with one to play. #18 was halved. Hummer became one of two finalists.

The winner of the other match was David Hetherington.

Thereby setting up the championship match, the winner of which would become the U.S. Amateur Champion. (Among the most prized trophies in all of golf.)

VISION 54
by Dudley Peters

The Participants

David Hetherington out of the Florida Atlantic University,

Vs.

and Henry Mueller of Briar Lakes Golf Club in Maryland.

Tomorrow. Tee Time - 8:00 AM (36 holes, to determine the Champion)

Cherry Hills Golf Club was expecting a lot of patrons for this match.

The next morning, both players started their warm-up routines at the driving range.

There was little talk, if any, between them. David's caddy was another FAU team player. His name was Ted Dodd.

Joanie and Ted met each other and talked for a few minutes, then went back to work.

After the driving range, they went to the chipping area and then the putting green. There, almost nothing was said by either player. Tee time was now 5 minutes away.

Tee time.

A tournament official held out the two cards, and David drew one. He would be hitting first.

After all of the introductions, David teed up his ball. He hit a very high and very long drive right down the middle, some 300 yards. It got a lot of applause.

Hummer grabbed his driver, teed up his ball, took a few practice swings, and stepped in; he connected. The ball flew high and long, landing in the fairway 330 yards from the tee. Again, there was applause. Both players birdied the first hole.

The $2^{nd}$ and $3^{rd}$ holes were halved. On #4. Hummer got into trouble with a shot running into the woods and stopping on some tree roots. He lost the hole; he was now 1 down.

On the very next hole, Hummer missed his birdie, and David made his. He was now 2-down. Then, on #6, a par 3, Hummer's tee ball landed just 2 feet from the cup. He won the hole. Down 1. On 7 & 8, both holes were halved. #9 was won by David, with a chip-in from 78 yards. He was in the lead 2-up over Hummer.

<u>The back nine.</u>

#10. David cut off the dog leg with a beautiful drive over the trees, leaving himself in the fairway 139 yards out. Hummer followed with a similar shot, leaving him with 141 yards to go. The hole was halved.

#11. David made a nice birdie to win the hole. He was now 3-up.

#12 & #13. Both holes were halved. Hummer asked Joanie, "What's your advice?"

"Well, there's nothing wrong with your game; we've just run into a buzz saw right now, but I'm not worried in the least. Right now, you are 3 down with 5 holes left to play. The way our opponent is playing, I think we must simply outplay him. He doesn't make many mistakes."

#14. Hummer made birdie, but so did David. He was still 3 down, with 4 to play.

#15. The hole was halved. David was now dormy.

#16. Hummer left his birdie putt on the edge of the hole. The hole was halved. David won the morning round 3 and 2.

In the club room, everyone tried to give Hummer support, telling him that he would still win. Hummer asked, "What did he shoot anyway?"

Joanie said, "Well, we don't know for sure, because of the few cedes we gave him, but I'd say, a 67."

"I shot a 70. I'm going to need to do a lot better this afternoon, for sure. I want this trophy especially bad."

"There's no doubt you can do it," said Joanie as they were eating lunch. Tee time was just an hour away. A little later, they headed out.

## The Final Round

by Dudley Peters

There was an abbreviated warm-up, and they were back on the tee.

Hole #1. David held the honors. He cut the dog's leg again and wound up 150 yards from the green. Hummer, also did the same, leaving himself 135 yards. Once more, they both halved the 1$^{st}$ hole.

Hummer then proceeds to birdie 3 holes in a row, #2,3,& 4, to bring the match back to where he was only down 1. (David birdied #4 also.)

Hole #5. Hummer reached the par 5 in two, and David was on in 3. Hummer's putt went in for eagle. The match was now even. On the very next hole, Hummer got into trouble and lost the hole. Down 1, again.

#7. Both players make a birdie, the hole is halved, still down 1.

#8. Hummer remembers Brad reminding him to stay left on this hole. His drive was nearly perfect, down the left-hand side. Both players were on in two, with birdie putts, and David was the first to go. He missed, and Hummer told him to pick it up. Hummer knew that this was a pivotal putt. It was critical at this time. He must make it. The putt was a 15-footer, downhill with little or no break. He took his time, went back below the hole again and looked, then went back to the ball and looked once more. He got ready and stroked it. The ball went into the center of the cup. A pretty big applause was to be heard by everyone. The match was now even.

#9. This hole was halved with pars. The match was now even with nine holes left.

### The Final Nine

#10. Hummer had the honors. He led off with a monster drive, well over 300 yards to the right center of the fairway. David's drive finished 40 yards behind him. David missed the green and wound up in the greenside bunker. Hummer dropped his wedge shot onto the green about 17 feet from the hole. David went down into the bunker and holed out the shot.

A huge round of applause broke out. Hummer felt like he had been hit in the stomach with a sledgehammer. He lost his mojo, temporarily. Joanie knew that Hummer would be taken aback if she didn't come up with the right words right then.

"Keep your mind on your game, and your game only. Pay no attention to anything else. Now go make this putt," she said.

Hummer lined up the putt and stroked the ball. It fell in on the edge of the hole. Another loud applause erupted. The match remained even.

#11 & #12. Both holes were halved with pars. Still even.

#13. After both drives and both approach shots, Hummer was away, facing a 22-footer. David had a 16-footer. Hummer looked at the line from both sides. He decided it would break 3 inches to the right. He got ready and hit it. It surprised everyone—there was no break. He then tapped in for a par.

David looked over his putt and knew that this was a critical point in time regarding this match, and the championship. He spent extra time on this one. When he was ready, he putted the ball and drained it. Hummer was now down 1 once more.

#14. They had both birdied this hole earlier today in this match. David got off another nice drive, Hummer followed with a good one as well. David hit his 7-iron to the center of the green, and Hummer hit his 8-iron 12 feet from the hole. It would be David putting first. David lined it up and putted, it stopped 3 inches short, and was ceded for par. Hummer then lined up his putt and made the stroke, he too came up short. His was ceded also. Still 1 down.

#15. This hole was halved with pars. Still 1 down.

#16. After two big drives on this par 5, David's ball was 1 yard in front of Hummer. Hummer got out his rescue club and swung it a few times then handed it back to Joanie and took the 3-wood. He caught it pure.

It flew all the way to the green, but was a long way away from the cup. David, had no hesitation, he grabbed his 3-wood, made a couple of practice swings, and connected. The ball went into the water on the left side. He then took a drop and chipped onto the green, but he was not close to the pin. Hummer putt this 30-plus footer as a lag putt, but amazingly, it went in for his second eagle of the round. Match was now back to even.

#17. This hole was halved with pars. The match remained even.

#18. Both players hit nice drives. David was next to play; he hit his 7-iron fairly close, about 8 or 9 feet from the hole. Then Hummer got ready to play his shot.

He selected his 8-iron and stroked it. It landed right beside David's ball. When they arrived at the green, a tournament official determined that David was away. David knew that this was what they call a "must putt." Both he and his caddy looked it over more than once, deciding on the line. David readied himself, then backed off. Ted handed him a towel, and he wiped his hands and forehead. He then readied himself once more. He stroked the ball, and it went into the center of the cup.

A huge round of applause burst out. It quickly quieted down as Hummer placed his ball down and picked up his marker. The ball was now in play. He looked it over; he had made a thousand putts like this before. He readied himself and stroked the ball. It reached the hole, caught the edge, made a complete circle, and somehow miraculously stayed out. David Hetherington became the U.S. Amateur Champion. Hummer earned the title of Runner-up.

Hummer wanted to get out of there as soon as possible. He was sick to his stomach, but he knew he had a commitment to stay and be a part of the closing ceremonies, which he did. He congratulated

David and gave him a firm handshake. At the ceremony, Hummer received a beautiful and hand-engraved plaque.

# Chapter 26

They all finally got back home. Hummer's Parents welcomed them both back, They had kept up with the golf tournament and were proud of both of them. His mother said: Don't worry dear, you will still always be a winner, as far as I'm concerned.

"Thanks, Mom."

Hummer went into his room and closed the door. It wasn't long before Joanie came in. "How are you feeling?"

"I should have never missed that putt. He showed me the line and everything. I still can't believe I missed it. I wanted it so bad."

"Some things go unexplained; this is one of those."

"I'm quitting golf, I feel just like I did when I lost all my money gambling on it."

"Well you're not quitting, I can tell you that."

"Yes, I am. No matter what you say."

"Do you know that you are invited to play in the Masters and the US Open?"

"What?"

"Here, read this." She hands him the papers from the USGA stating his eligibility. "Holy Smokes," he immediately perks up.

"Hey, Joanie, we have got to get prepared for this."

"I know, I know."

Two weeks later, Hummer got a certified letter from the USGA. In it, it said that, with his performance of scoring a sanctioned 62 at Cherry Hills

Golf Club during the US Amateur Tournament, along with being the Runner-up, The USGA shall afford him a Temporary USGA Tour card for two official tournaments, the upcoming Valero Texas Open in Houston, the week before the Masters, and The Zurich Classic of New Orleans, in late April.

Hummer re-read the letter in its entirety; he couldn't wait to show it to Joanie.

Something else came to him. He needed to tell Tommy and Brad right away about this.

Brad was the first to react. "Hummer, this is the best possible news you could get. You will be able to play in a PGA Tour event right before the Masters. This is great news. We must get to work on this immediately."

Tommy called. "This is great news! I'm very proud of you. Let me know if you need anything from me. I'm all in concerning you, Joanie, and Brad."

"Thank you, Tommy."

Joanie and Hummer told their parents that night at the diner table about the invitation to play in the PGA's Texas Open. Both parents wished him success and stated that they would not be in a position to go to Texas to watch him play. They simply couldn't afford it.

After dinner, there was a fruitful and factual conversation with Joanie about the future. Hummer started practicing, and every day, he hit buckets of balls. He was on the driving range, the putting green, the practice bunkers, the chipping area, stroke after stroke. He would play rounds with Mike too. Practice, practice, practice, and more practice. Yes,

Hummer was very serious now about everything. He felt good and fit. The Valero Texas Open now was only 1 month away.

# **Chapter 27**

Professional debut.

The Texas Open at San Antonio

The Oaks Course, par 72.

*The Valero **Texas Open**, first played in 1922, is the 3rd oldest PGA TOUR Tournament. It's only younger than the Western Open (1899) and Canadian Open (1904). If you include the U.S. Open (1895), managed by the USGA, and the PGA Championship (1916)*

All of Hummer's close golfing supporters agreed it would be an excellent site for his debut. Brad Davis told Hummer the course fit his game nicely, the others all agreed.

Hummer signed the invitation, committing to play, and sent it back. He got the approval notice. He was in.

Tommy made all of the travel arrangements as well as other accommodations. He also informed Hummer and reminded him about the contract his lawyers were currently drawing up for the franchise.

PGA Tournaments generally hold, Monday and Tuesday, for unscheduled practice rounds, Wednesday is the Pro-am, (normally big donors, sponsors, or VIPs, that pay to play a round with the pros.)

by Dudley Peters

Thursday finally got there, Hummer's tee time was set for 11:10 AM. He did not know any of the players in his threesome. He only knew them from TV or golf magazines.

He got all of his practice routines completed. He was ready to play. Joanie checked the bag. She put in two new ice-cold waters. They were ready.

They took the tee, the pro's introduced themselves to one another. Each, was then announced to the spectators, just before they would hit their first Drive. Hummer was hitting third.

When it was his turn, he decided to hit the three-wood, it was a nice drive. This hole was quite short for a par 4. When he hit his 9-iron to the green it was very nice also.

Hummer, one-putted for birdies on the first two holes, both par 4's, from very short distances, it was two easy birdies on two rather short par 4 holes.

On the $3^{rd}$ hole, a par 5, he hit the green with his second shot from 190 yards out, but the speed of the green helped the ball to roll off into a greenside bunker. He got there, stepped into the bunker, looked over the lie, it was okay. Joanie handed him his sand iron. He blasted the ball out. It then rolled toward the hole, kept running, then stopped some 10 feet past the hole.

It started raining a bit harder now. Just before he was to putt for his $3^{rd}$ consecutive birdie, the rain wasn't hard enough to stop play, however.

Hummer was facing a 10-foot, 2-inch, up-hiller, with just a little break to the right. The crowd had been growing around this trio of players. They leaned into the restraining ropes and quietly watched as Hummer putt his ball, with perfect speed, into the center of the cup.

A rather large round of applause and noise echoed over the area. More spectators joined the already oversized group of spectators. Hummer had now birdied the first three holes.

The crowd had a surreal feeling that something special was going to happen today. It was in the air. No, it was more than that. All of the pre-tournament hype, had the gallery alerted about this first-time starter, This rookie, Henry Muller. He had recently shot a score of 62, to earn the title of US Amateur Runner-up. Right now, he was stunning and delivering excitement to the growing crowd that was anxiously looking on.

Hole #4 was a par 3, 196 yards, with an oversized, undulating green. Hummer had the honors, he asked Joanie for his 5-iron. He took several practice swings, paused, and then asked for his 6-iron, which he had pictured in his mind, hitting short of the pin and landing on top of a swell on the green so that the ball would roll to the left and toward the hole. It would be a safer shot than going right at the pin. He needed to make sure he didn't go over the back. It was a highly elevated green and there was trouble back there.

He then took a few practice swings. Joanie handed him a towel. After drying his hands, he took a series of practice swings, then stepped in and connected. The ball went very high and very straight. The crowd stretched to watch, as it hit the green on the top of the rise and ran down towards the hole, stopping some 8 inches from the hole. "it's going to be another Birdie," the crowd roared. After he made the putt, the crowd roared again.

Hole #5 was a par four, 469 yds. It was a severe dog leg left. The hole was long and had heavy rough, and dense woods on both sides, it had a narrow fairway, as well as strategically placed bunkers, and there was a pond just in front of the green with the ground running down toward it. It was one of the 2 hardest holes to make par on the golf course. This hole was one of those difficult types of holes, where if you make par, you felt good walking off the green.

Hummer looked at his yardage book, checking the distance to the dog's leg. He also looked down the fairway to see just how tall the trees were, should he decide to hit over them. It was 256 yards to the beginning of the dog's leg. His thinking was: Should I draw it around the corner, or go over the top?

He asked Joanie what she thought. She said, "You've got a great round going, I would play safe on this particular hole. It's one of the hardest holes out here."

"Okay, hand me the 3-wood." He swung it several times, getting the feel he wanted.

VISION 54
by Dudley Peters

The rain started to pick up again as he was preparing to play. He visualized a big rolling hook-draw for the shot. He thought for just a moment about hitting the driver but quickly decided to stay with the 3-wood. Hummer teed the ball low, then readied himself for the stroke. He took a few more practice swings than usual, then stepped in position. The huge crowd watched as Hummer connected once more with another pure stroke.

The huge gallery applauded loudly for the golf shot they had just seen. The ball followed the middle of the fairway around the dog leg and ended up in the left-center fairway in a perfect, flat lie, 310 yards from the tee. He now left himself with only 158 yards to the pin. When it was His turn to play, the crowd of spectators strained in every way to watch the next shot.

He swung the wedge and sent the ball extremely high into the air, on a great line, it landed and spun towards the hole just 12 feet away. Again, the crowd erupted with excitement and applause. When it was Hummer's turn to putt, everyone could feel it. Everyone was nervous, hoping to see it drop. He struck the putt. Again, with perfect speed, it went into the center of the cup. The crowd frenzy got louder and more excited. Both of the pros he was playing with gave him a "thumbs up."

Hole #6 was another par five, 581 yds. With a narrow fairway with woods on the right all the way and a large lake on the left with a slight dog leg to the left, plus everything was leaning left and running downhill towards the lake. The two fairway bunkers were strategically located. The one on the left began at 250 yards from the tee, and the one on the right began at 267 yards from the tee. It would take a 320-yard carry, to make it over either of these two bunkers.

Hummer was again hitting first; he asked for his 3-wood, and he swung it a few times to get the feel he wanted; he turned and looked down the fairway for a moment, then handed the club back to Joanie. "I'll take the driver," he said. Everyone could hear the murmurs from the crowd.

Hummer proceeded to smash a mammoth drive, high over the left bunker with a mini fade. It cleared the bunker easily and landed in the fairway 330 yards in the air, the run-out added another 21 yards. He was left with 230 yards to the pin.

The crowd had, at this point had swollen to a huge mass of spectators, golf enthusiasts, and sports writers. The Tournament Officials were having trouble with crowd control, they were spilling onto the fairway and other parts of the course where they were not allowed.

They all wanted to see if this rookie could score six consecutive birdies on the first six holes. There was electricity in the air, the crowd could feel it.

Normally, the opening day of any regular tour stop was the day that the fewest ticketholders attended, and with today being rainy, even less spectators were there, the guess was 25, to 35 thousand.

VISION 54
by Dudley Peters

Hummer looked over his lie, the ball was sitting up nicely, but there was some mud on its left side, also the lie was a little bit downhill. He asked Joanie for the 4-iron. He swung it a few times. He then asked her for a new dry glove. She took the old one, then handed him the new one along with a dry towel. He wiped everything off and stepped up to the ball, took two more practice swings, and then connected.

It was a wonderful shot, high and long and with perfect distance. It came to a stop 14 feet from the hole, pin high. The crowd again roared. Hummer felt the adrenaline rush through his veins and to his brain. His two playing partners acknowledged the shot. When the golfers walked onto the green, the ball positions, dictated that Hummer would be putting last. He marked his ball and handed it to Joanie, he was trying his best to be calm and steady while waiting for his turn to putt.

While still waiting his turn, he looked over the eagle putt. It was perfectly straight, but with the grain at 90°. He made a mental note and then waited. He placed his ball down and picked up the ball marker.

He walked to the other side of the hole and looked for the line he would use. He then got into position. The growing crowd became virtually silent. He struck the putt.

by Dudley Peters

The ball made an unexpected move to the right, caught the lip of the hole, made a circle, and somehow stayed out. Hummer tapped it in for his sixth consecutive birdie. The crowd went into frenzy mode.

Word traveled, and the fairly large crowd watching Him had now grown even bigger, they started forcing their way forward to get a better look, at what was happening. The restraining ropes were being overly tested. The rain became a little more steady now, but not heavy enough to stop play.

Hummer's playing group was now on the next tee.

Hole #7 was another par three, 186 yards. It was an elevated green with two very deep bunkers on either side of the green. The slope was designed for balls to run off the green if they got anywhere near the frog hair or fringe. The wetness had become a bit of a problem now. The club grips were wet and slippery, new gloves would get wet quickly, raindrops were dripping from the bill of the golf hats, etc. They pressed on.

Hummer asked for the 6 iron. Joanie toweled it off. He teed up the ball, toweled off the grips again, and stepped in. He took more than his normal amount of practice swings. The rain had not discouraged the crowd of spectators in the least, they knew they were watching history being made. They could feel it.

All of a sudden, in an instant, the rain weakened, it became very light, hardly noticeable, the sky brightened. Hummer stepped back, went over to his bag, and asked for his seven iron. Joanie said, "Are you sure?" She handed it to him. He went back to the tee, leaned over pushed his ball a wee bit lower, stepped up, took a couple of practice swings, and then connected, the ball just barely made the front portion of the green and started rolling, it gathered speed and ran off the green and into the front left bunker. The huge crowd quieted down and emitted a moan.

Joanie said, "This is no problem for you, you have done this plenty of times."

"I should have stayed with the six."

"Maybe, maybe not, you'll never know. Right now, we need to make par."

The mass of spectators were eerily quiet right now. Hummer walked down into the bunker, it was extremely wet, but there were no puddles. He took a stance, even though he was nowhere even close to being ready to make a stroke. His feet were about 5 ft. below the putting surface. He could easily see the hole about 30 feet away. He felt he knew where to land the ball with a little spin to help stop it fairly close to the pin.

The rain was still light. He asked for a towel, and Joanie handed him a dry one. He wiped off the grip. He stood there just looking at the hole for a long 20 seconds. He took his stance. The crowd stretched and craned in anticipation of the shot. Hummer slid the sand iron under the ball, taking the perfect amount of sand with it.

VISION 54
by Dudley Peters

The ball hit the green just above the hole, made one hop, spun backward a bit, and then ever so slowly fell into the cup.

Not just the spectators, but the Radio and TV announcers went crazy. They were all agog, with what they just saw.

They became energized like never before. "Unbelievable." Was the word being used and heard all over the sports world? The excitement of the moment was unparalleled. The news spread, now even most of the social media outlets had started covering the event. People were following with their phones. It was like the whole world was watching.

Hummer had now miraculously birdied 7 consecutive holes. He was leading the tournament by 5 shots, he was not only the talk of the Tournament, he was the talk of the golfing world, and then some. When the scoreboards revealed the 7 consecutive birdies, approximately 90% of the patrons made their way to join the already bulging crowd.

Hole #8 was a par 4, 430 yards and uphill. The hole was a straight-away hole with a narrow fairway. They had let the rough grow to

5 inches tall. There were two pot bunkers also, that needed to be avoided at all costs. Hummer was interested only in the far one. He asked Joanie,

"How far to the far bunker?"

"280."

He pulled out his driver and took off the head cover.

"Are you sure?" She asked.

"No, I'm going to need a little luck with this one. The uphill effect could cause trouble."

"That's right, your ball will come down early, I was just about to remind you of that."

"Right."

"Why not the 3-wood then?"

No answer.

He grabbed a towel from under the umbrella and wiped the grip and his glove.

"You want a new glove?"

"How many are left?"

"Three."

"I'll wait, but hand me a dry towel."

He stayed with the driver, toweled off his glove again, Teed up the ball, and stepped in. Took 2 practice swings, then connected. Once more, the strike was pure.

It looked as though it was headed for the pot bunker; it hit the ground running, it rolled by the bunker, missing going into it by no more than a foot. It rolled past and stopped 140 yards from the center of the green.

The large crowd roared. They had now begun roaring after any and every shot. None of the broadcasters could recall that happening ever before.

Both of his playing companions were having trouble here. One was in the heavy rough, and the other one was in the first pot bunker. Each had to lay up. It was now Hummer's turn.

He pulled out the wedge, swung it several times, then handed it to Joanie. She stuck out the 9-iron; he took it, swung it several times, and stepped in. The mass of spectators was doing everything possible to get a better position. Pushing, shoving, squirming, craining, stretching, and everything else to get a better position. It was a lot of commotion.

The drizzle now had a few big rain drops mixed in, everything was wet and getting wetter.

The crowd noise lessened a bit. Hummer just took one more practice swing and made the stroke. It flew high and true. It moved a little to the left, and landed on the green, then stopped 11 feet above the hole.

The crowd once more roared and clapped, the broadcasters joined in with words of praise. There was excitement everywhere.

It took a while for the players to squeeze their way through the throng, and finally reach the green. It was like a mob scene.

Hummer marked his ball and tossed it to Joanie. He took a couple of steps back and eyed the line. It was going to break right a little, maybe 3 inches, he thought.

It now was his turn to putt, He placed the ball down, picked up the marker, and prepared to putt.

He intended to play it 3 inches to the left. Joanie moved in towards him; he backed off.

"What is it?" He asked.

"With it being a little bit downhill, plus with the grain, along with the wetness, it might not break as much as it looks. I was just making sure you have all the information you need to hole this putt."

He didn't say anything; he assumed his stance and stroked it. The ball goes into the hole on the inside edge of the cup.

Everyone went nuts again. It was so loud, that you couldn't hear yourself talk, you could only clap and roar. The media was having a field day.

Hummer had now birdied 8 consecutive holes.

Hole # 9 was a drivable par 4, 349 yards. It had two extremely high bunkers on either side of the small green. The opening to the green was only 8 yards wide. Around the green, the rough was 5 inches tall. This hole was troublesome if you tried to drive it. The hole had already produced a number of bogeys.

Hummer pondered about this hole. It didn't feel right. It was not a yardage he liked, plus he could see the trouble.

The way the fairway was laid out, the only safe iron shot would be a 9 or 8-iron. Also, starting about 180 yards out, there was a small, marked-off, environmental area, then there was hard pan, on both sides, with sloping shoulders leading right into the woods.

Joanie asked, "What do you think?"

"Either 8-iron or driver," he said.

"What about the 3-wood?" she said, "you could hit it past all that trouble, be short of the bunkers, and leave yourself an easy chip."

"Hand me the 3. I like it."

The green cleared, Hummer teed up his ball, looked at the fairway for a long time, took several practice swings, and then connected. The ball flew high and long with a little fade, hit the ground, and stopped 5 yards from the right bunker. The applause, the yelling, and the roars were ear-shattering.

The media was mesmerized, there were no words they could use to embellish what was unfolding.

When it was Hummer's turn, he hit the chip shot up, it hit the pin, almost went in, and stopped 20 inches from the hole. After the tap in, an all-out frenzy went into full bloom. It was a 27 on the front nine.

Nine consecutive birdies, a real live miracle. The threesome was swarmed, they couldn't move. They were part of the mob.

More Police were called in, the threesome was happy to see them. They finally started to slowly move.

# Chapter 28

### <u>The Back Nine</u>

Hole # 10 was another par 4, a dog leg right, 410 yards. There was nothing special about this hole. It was a simple dog leg hole. It has two Regular greenside bunkers and wider than normal fairways. It looked like a piece of cake to Hummer. He decided to cut the dog leg. He took the driver, made several practice strokes, stepped in, and connected. The strike was less than pure. The trajectory was not as high as normal. It hit the top of a tree, bounced backward to the left, and landed in the rough, leaving a long approach shot of 225 yards.

The horde of spectators moaned. It was an unexpected situation for them. They were stunned, but there was still a lot of noise of support and faith. They were whole-heartedly behind him.

He was away. He looked over the situation, the distance, and the lie. He was mad at himself for the miss-hit, but he knew he must put that behind him immediately.

He grabbed the rescue club from the bag and took several practice swings. Joanie says, "You have this shot, go for it."

He took a few extra practice swings and stepped in. This time, the shot was pure. It sailed toward the green and stopped where his ball was on the green, but tight up against the edge of the frog hair, some 19 feet from the hole. It would be a very difficult putt.

## VISION 54
### by Dudley Peters

The next player in the threesome only had 150 yards to the pin. He hit a 8-iron. It landed and stopped on the frog-hair fairly close to Hummer's ball. Undoubtedly, it would be a big help to Hummer, showing him the speed and break.

When the time came, Hummer carefully watched his opponent putt. He followed it intensely; he saw both the speed and line. The ball stopped a foot short and about 4 to 5 inches on the low side, if it had got there. It showed Hummer everything he needed to know.

The massive crowd pressed in, it was very noisy. Hummer placed the ball down, picked up the marker, and got ready. He putted. Then, with perfect speed, it went into the center of the cup. The noise was indescribable, it sounded like a bomb had went off.

Everyone was involved. Joanie and Hummer just looked at each other. Then, they tried to force their way forward towards the next tee. It was going to be tough getting through. Finally, they made it. Hummer had now birdied 10 consecutive holes.

The players started noticing that it was getting a bit difficult getting to the next tee, because of the many spectators crammed together in the paths and walkways.

Hole#11 was a par 3, 198 yards. It looked like an island green, but the lake didn't go all around to the back. It had one huge bunker on the left side. The pin was middle-back. Hummer decided to play his shot, right at the hole.

Some of the ground control officials were waving the Quiet signs. They went unheeded. Amid all of the noise, he hit the 6-iron. The shot was a little right, and short. He now faced an uphill 13-foot putt with a left break. When it was his turn to putt, he took extra time to decide on the break.

He putted. The putt just barely got to the hole, it slowly rode the right edge of the hole, stopped, and then fell back into the cup.

The huge crowd of people went into frenzy mode. They were not only loud, but they were berserk acting. It took a great effort for the 3 golfers to reach the next tee. It started to rain a little harder now. Again, it was a task for the players to make their way through the crowd to get to the next tee.

Hole #12 was a par 4, 405 yards in length. It was rated as one of the easiest holes on the course. After the threesome had negotiated their way through the mass of people, they finally got to the tee. Still, the noise was extremely loud and uncontrollable. Hummer's 3-wood and 9-iron had him on the green in regulation.

The siren went off just as Hummer marked his ball; he and Joanie headed for the clubhouse. His mark was just 14 feet from the pin and 14 feet from his 12th consecutive birdie. He was now 11 under par.

He had already broken the old record of 8 birdies in a row, set by Seve Ballesteros and Ian Woosnam in 1985.

All of the broadcasters were now focused on Henry Muller, as well as sports writers and others that crowded in. No one wanted to miss seeing what was going to happen today. After all, history was already being rewritten.

After 30 minutes of waiting, Tournament officials called off play for the day. The announcement said: "Play would resume at 6:30 AM tomorrow morning."

To the TV media, radio broadcasters, ticket sales companies, and other vendors, this was a huge bonus for them.

Phone calls started coming in from people all over, who wanted tickets for tomorrow's completion of round 1 and the rest of the tournament. By 6 pm, they were estimating that there would be over 76,000 ticket holders for the rest of the tournament, maybe even 100,000.

This morning's round had close to 35 thousand spectators, a little short of what had been expected, mostly due to the rainy forecast.

The sportscasters were beginning to talk about Annika Sorenstam's prediction of a "54" as being the greatest achievement, obtainable in all of golf. It was on most observers' minds right now.

This fourteen-footer Hummer was yet to putt, but it might very well be the most watched putt in golf history, even though it would be struck tomorrow morning at 6:30 AM CDT. That would be 7:30 AM New York time and 4:30 AM California time. In Europe, it would be in the fore noon of the morning. The entire golfing world would be tuned in, for sure.

The main media used this time to add affiliates into the stream, it was a money-making bonanza for them. Ads started popping up everywhere, promoting the event. Calling it "THE MIRICLE OF GOLF IN REAL TIME."

Joanie and Hummer were back at the hotel. They were watching the TV. The Texas Open was on nearly every channel. Hummer's name was heard over and over again until your ears got numb.

One broadcaster was saying, "Eleven birdies in a row, and now a putt for twelve. It's never been done, and should he make this 14-foot putt, could he, would he, or will he, do the impossible?"

"We will all find out tomorrow morning."

The whole story is right out of the Book of Miracles. A rookie golfer, playing in his first tournament and doing this. It's simply astounding.

Sportscasters got wind of other famous golfers, including Annika Sorenstam, who had flown in last night to watch today's finish. They quickly aired this information to the public.

Sportscasters and newsmen were hustling to find out some inside information about this 19-year-old phenom from Rockville, Maryland.

VISION 54
by Dudley Peters

They managed to find out that he had tied the course record of 64 at Briar Lakes Golf Club at the age of 16. They discovered that also, at 16, he won a Pro-am in Maryland with a 64 score.

They knew he carded a 62 at the US Amateur at the age of 18.

They also discovered that he was natural. He never attended any golf school or had taken any paid lessons.

Joanie turned the TV down and asked Hummer about dinner. "What do you feel like?"

"I'm not sure."

"Would you like for me to go get us some fast food?"

"That's a good idea. I think I'd like a bacon burger from Burger King with Onion rings on the side."

"Great, there's one right up the street, are you ready for it now?"

"Yes."

"Let me ask you something: Are you sore anywhere? If you are, I can help with that. I brought some sports lotion with me."

"I think I'm okay. My problem is that putt that's waiting for me in the morning. That's going to be bothering me all night, I just know it."

"I brought your golf bag to my room. After we eat, I'm going to get them all cleaned and dried up. Then I'm bringing you the putter for you to sleep with."

"Sleep with? Are you nuts?"

"Yes, yes I am, just like Einstein," she said, then she added, "we are going to the putting green early tomorrow, where you will do your normal putting routine, then 10 minutes before we resume play, you will be back on the putting green, and we will putt nothing but 14 footers until they call us."

"Okay, sounds like a plan."

"I'll be right back, I'm headed to Burger King. I have the money."

Meanwhile, the Tournament officials were having an emergency meeting at the clubhouse, regarding the impending crowd of spectators expected.

How to handle them was the question. This meeting would be a long one. Every person there had no beneficial, or positive answer.

Back at the hotel, Joanie was talking about the early start tomorrow and what time they should get to the course.

"My normal warm-up routine takes about 45 minutes, but it can be altered, if we are pressed."

"Okay, we'll get there at five. I'll wake you at 4:15. We better get some rest now. See you in the morning."

They went to bed. Surprisingly, Hummer slept fairly well. Joanie. Not so much. She tossed and turned and was awake most of the night. 4:15 arrived. She went in and woke him. They prepared to leave. It was ten of five when they got there. Unbelievable, but true, the golf course was already jammed packed. People were everywhere.

Hummer got spotted. A swarm of ticket holders moved in on him. Phones and cameras were clicking like crazy. People were asking for pictures and autographs. Hummer did not know what to do. Joanie took command; she had to. She pushed their way under the ropes to a better, safer, and somewhat more open space.

The sun peeped over the horizon, and the forecast was perfect. Sunny with little or no wind, temperature low 80's.

Just before starting his routine, one single-ground reporter had managed to get beside Hummer. He asked, "Hummer, are you going to make the putt?"

Joanie heard him and said to herself, *what a stupid question.* Then Hummer replied, "I'm going to give it my best."

He then tried to concentrate. The crowd noise was a big hindrance. After hitting his irons and woods, they moved to the practice green. A huge horde of golf fans were there just to watch Hummer and see how many birdies he would make. Plus to see in person, this 14 foot attempt.

It seemed like no time had passed when Hummer found himself on the 12th green. He found his ball marker, he stood a couple of feet behind it. Right then, he remembered some TV announcer saying last night that This 14-foot putt would be the most-watched putt in golf history. Hummer wished he could think about something else. The horn blew.

Hummer was putting second. No ball on the green would help him with the line or speed of his putt. His playing opponent putted, it went by the hole some 4 feet.

The mass of people started jostling for better positions, some were downright rude. Everyone did whatever they could to see this putt.

Hummer placed the ball down, picked up the marker then stepped back. A rush of adrenaline was released throughout his body and brain. He could see more clearly than ever before, he stepped in.

For the first time since the 6th hole yesterday, when the uncontrollable roars and noise began, the huge horde of spectators went quiet.

Hummer took one last look at the hole, then stroked it. The ball headed toward the hole, it rolled with perfect speed and went in.

The eruption began, and the roar and applause came from everywhere, it was epic. Crowd control turned impossible.

Hummer had just birdied 12 consecutive holes. Now he had to somehow get to the next tee without injury. The spectators were jammed together, they had no choice of which way they went, they were like they were glued together.

Joanie and Hummer started jostling their way. Some of the crowd tried to help. And did.

Finally, they reached Hole #13, a 505-yard, par 5. This hole was a casual bending hole, it was like the shape of a banana, with the bend turning right. There was a single large pine tree in the center of the fairway 178 yards in front of the tee. It's 2-foot wide trunk had been pruned up high, to about 30 feet before the first limb. The trees' total height was 75 feet. There were no fairway bunkers on this hole, but there was a lake that stretched all the way across the front of the green. Another thing, there were 20 yards of grass between the back of the lake and the green.

With all of the loud noise going on, Joanie got right up close to his ear and asked, "Which side of the tree are you aiming for?"

"I'm going over the top."

He teed it up high, took a few practice swings, and stepped into position. He readied himself and swung. The ball flew a little left of the tree, very high, then started to fade. It landed in the fairway 305 yards from the tee.

When it was his turn to play, he had 200 yards to the green. He stood behind his ball and looked at the green, he decided on an easy 5-iron. He struck it. The ball cleared the lake but landed in the grass in front of the green. The illusion of the lake appearing to be right up against the green had caused Hummer to misjudge how hard to swing the 5-iron. Even the moan of the crowd was deafening.

After both of his opponents were on the green, Hummer asked for his lob wedge. He readied himself and made the stroke; the ball landed, took one bounce, and stopped. It was 2 feet from the hole. The huge mass of spectators went crazy, the TV announcers also. Everyone knew that it was going to be 13 in a row. The world was watching too. When it was his turn to putt, the crowd didn't even attempt to quieten down. He putted the ball straight into the hole. Pandemonium! Spread.

They now had to somehow worm their way through to the next tee. They made it without injury.

Hole #14 was a par 3, playing 188 yards, pin in the back. Hummer asks for the 6-iron.  "Are you sure?"

"What are you thinking?" asked Hummer.

"I'm thinking about you going over the green. I would rather see you in the middle of the green."

"Thanks, Joanie, good idea, I'll baby the 6."

The TV announcers were struggling to find different descriptive words. The massive crowd was clamoring for position. It was noisy and rough. Up by the green, They broke through the rope and were around part of the green. The ground crew did their best.  Hummer wasn't sure if he should hit the shot. There's never been anything even close, as to what was happening.

VISION 54
by Dudley Peters

Hummer teed the ball low this time, took several practice swings, and stepped in. He again readied himself and then connected. The ball hit the front portion of the green, in a soft damp area, and got almost no roll, leaving him with a long putt of about 23 feet, all uphill. He would be the first to play.

He walked all the way up past the hole and eyed the line needed. He then went back to the ball and eyed the line again. He decided the break would be about 18 inches. The world was watching, the enormous crowd muscled in. The noise was still there, loud as ever. He moved in, got ready to putt, then walked away.

He re-assessed the putt, considering how hard to hit it and the line needed to make it. Again, he stepped in, and like magic, the crowd noise abated some. He struck the putt; it headed toward the hole and started to turn. It made it all the way to the right edge, then dropped.

The roar was louder than ever; the crowd was going berserk. The broadcasters were beside themselves in euphoria, and the world was excited.

The task of getting to the next tee was now at hand. Two guards were helping them get through. They squeezed and forged ahead. All of the media people were completely hyped up, frenzied. The world was now on edge, watching. A rookie pro golfer was making golf history.

Hole #15 was a par 4, with a length of 401 yards. Hummer asked for the driver.

Joanie said, "Why not the 3-wood? It gets narrow way down there."

"You are right, I'll take the 3-wood, and thanks," he replied.

He made the strike; it was pure, once again. The ball flew high and long, right down the middle. He had only 126 yards left to the pin, one of his favorite distances. After both of the other pros were on the green, Hummer got ready for his approach. He took a few practice swings, stepped in, and connected. The ball was high and on line. It landed behind the pin and spun back to just a mere 20 inches from the cup.

The already noisy crowd went crazy again, as did the announcers. The whole world was caught up in what was unfolding right before their eyes. Hummer had just birdied 15 consecutive holes in the Texas Open.

There were no words to describe this that hadn't already been used a hundred times. Getting to the next tee was now the challenge. The mass of people was impenetrable. Nobody could move. Getting to the next tee would take time. Eventually, they got there.

Hole #16. Par 5, 522 yards. Dogleg left. Hummer asked Joanie, "Should I cut the corner?"

"It's a little longer than the last one, and the trees are taller," she replied.

"So?" he asked.

"I like a safer play. I want you to hit a nice drive out there with a little draw."

"3-wood or driver?" he asked.

"The one you like best," she answered.

He selected the 3-wood and teed the ball low. He took several practice strokes and stepped in. He swung and connected. Once again, he caught it pure. It reached the dogleg, drew around, then came to a stop. He had a good lie and 252 yards to the pin.

When it became his turn to play, he asked for the 4-iron. Joanie handed it to him. He readied himself and swung. It was not a pure shot; he struck high on the clubface, and the ball came up short.

He was 15 yards short of the undulating green and 22 yards from the cup. The noisy crowd groaned but remained loud. It was Hummer's turn to play. There was one knoll that he definitely needed to navigate. A flop shot might work, but a chip and run was the best way to go.

"Joanie, what do you like from here, flop or chip and run?"

"Flop."

"Hand me the lob."

VISION 54
by Dudley Peters

He takes a lot of practice swings. Then takes a bunch more. With everyone cramming, stretching, pushing, watching, and doing everything else possible to see the shot. He stroked it. It was a perfect strike, the ball popped up and came down right beside the hole. Mayhem broke out.

With his tap-in, it was now 16 consecutive birdies.

It was like no one was in charge. It was near riot conditions everywhere. In the TV broadcaster's booth, Annika had made her way there. She joined in with the announcers, even the Golden Bear, himself had called in, Tiger Woods, too. Top Players around the world were calling in. The Texas Open itself had many world-ranked, top golfers playing there. Unbelievably, there were only small groups with them. Yes, the main action was now at the 17th hole. The main scoreboard had a sign that read; 16 in, with 2 to go! The players, somehow, reached the tee intact.

Hole #17. Par 4, this was a short hole, only 389 yards. It had two large fairway bunkers and two steep greenside bunkers. Also, there was a small pond that came in to play, in front of the green. Hummer was deciding how close he wanted to be from the hole after his drive. He asks Joanie. "How far to the lake?"

"290," she said.

"What do you think?"

"Go 275, at the most."

He then asked for the rescue club.

"You sure, I was thinking 4-iron?"

"Rescue."

"Okay, I like it," She said.

He teed it low, took several practice swings, stepped in, and connected. The ball took off like a rocket toward the target. It stopped 15 yards in front of the lake, leaving him 21 yards to the pin. The roar from the mass of people was deafening.

Now, just getting down to the ball was going to be a challenge. People were not able to move. Crowd control had been dissolved some time ago. It was everyone on his own. You almost had to hack your way through, like in the jungle. Everyone there wanted to see this happen in real life and claim that they were there.

The fans had been seeing this for 2 days now, to them they felt like the birdie here would be automatic. Even though, there was an inner nervousness felt by them all.

Then, after forging their way through the crowd. Hummer was figuring out the shot. He took the lob wedge and swung it several times to get a good feel. He took his stance, swung twice more, then connected. He didn't catch it like he wanted, it flew over the pin and stopped 12 feet away. That didn't matter to the gigantic crowd. They roared anyway. Hummer was taken aback. He immediately remembered the putt he missed at the US Amateur.

The adrenaline was gone, until Joanie stepped close to his ear and said,

"Hummer, look at me. I believe in you."

Right then, he breathed new life. He struck the putt, it went toward the hole, then fell in. Bedlam everywhere.

The main scoreboard sign now read "17 in 1 to go!"

The massive crowd did their best to try and make an opening for them, it helped a little, but not much. It was still difficult to move forward. After a while, they got through.

The 18th hole and surrounding clubhouse area were now a sea of uncontrollable golf fans. The emergency vehicles and medical tents were busy with patrons needing attention. All of the vendors were nearly out of goods to sell, it was as close as you could get to mass utopia.

Broadcasters were out of new descriptive words. Now, with the whole world watching, the focus turned to the 18th hole of the Valero Texas Open.

Hole #18. A difficult par 4, at 470 yds. All the way down the left, just 15 yards off the fairway, is a wide running creek that meanders most of the way to the hole, then it cuts across, separating the fairway as it runs in front of the green and into the woods. The hole is rated and proven to be the hardest hole on the golf course.

The strategically placed fairway bunkers are on both sides of the narrow fairway, with dense woods on the right.

Hummer was aware of where he was and what had happened so far in the tournament, and the massive crowd knew exactly what was at stake. Hummer stood on the Tee, waiting for clearance to drive. He was trying to collect himself when an odd, strange feeling came over him, this strange feeling took over, then consumed all of his attention, it was a feeling he had never experienced before, it overwhelmed him.

Joanie was the first to notice. She leaned over and asked, "Are you all right?"  There was no reply. A look came forth from Hummer's face, as he welled up. His mind thought of only one thing, and one thing only. Family. He wanted his family to be proud of him. He didn't look into the crowd for them because he knew they weren't there. So he looked only at Joanie. Then, for just a moment, he looked out into the crowd and saw them. His Mother, Father, and big sister were there in the crowd cheering for him. It was all he could do, not to cry. Instead, He looked back at Joanie. Like always, she read him like a book. "Yep, she said, they're here."

The TV camera zoomed in close, and the huge throng of spectators leaned in and pushed their way, testing the ropes to get a closer look in any way they could to see his face. The golfing fans all over the world were glued to their TV's watching as history was being made for all to see.

Joanie went into the bag, retrieved a bottle of water and handed it to Hummer. She then said, "Hummer, take a minute and collect yourself, take a swig of water."

He did.

Joanie then put her hands on both of his shoulders. She looked him straight into his eyes. "We need birdie!"

She deliberately paused for a long moment, then said: "GO GET IT !"

Hummer had the honors, he cleared his mind and concentrated only on this next shot. All of his abilities were to

be brought forth. He knew the three-wood would leave him within 170 to 175 yards to the green, the driver would leave him with 140 yards, but the fairway narrowed dramatically, as it got closer to the green, which could cause a problem. He asked for the three-wood. He swung it several times, then he asked Joanie what she thought.

"I think either one will do, your call."

He only hesitated for a second, he would hit the three- wood.

Joanie saw some of the masses still in the fairway. They had still not been cleared yet. She moved in close to Hummer, looked at him, and said, "You do know Hummer, exactly what's happening here, right? You have already made and are making history. I had a thought come to me a moment ago. I want to share it with you. I read a slogan-type statement in a book somewhere. I believe it applies to you at this moment. It read, "Bound by Determination and Fueled by Adrenaline. I believe that's you; I believe that's always been you, I believe that's you right now.  So, GO GET IT !  I want that birdie."

The fairway finally cleared for the most part, and Hummer stepped in and teed up his ball. The immense crowd was at least 25 to 40 deep, thousands and thousands of ticket holders were right there, all testing the ropes and cringing to see him. Virtually every volunteer and crowd control official were here with this threesome. TV cameras were everywhere. The world was watching.

The horde of people ahead cleared most of the fairway on both sides, it was time for Him to hit his drive.

Hummer stepped up, reached down, and re-teed his ball, he moved it about a foot more toward the left side of the tee box, then, after a few practice swings, he stepped in. The crowd tried to get quiet. They didn't. It was just so many there, any source of silence was unattainable.

Hummer connected, it was a beautiful drive, almost 300 yards, center cut. It came to rest 172 yards from the pin, with a perfect lie. The roar from the throngs of spectators was deafening. His two playing companions were also cheering for him.

Both of his playing companions decided to lay-up with their second shots. It was now time for Hummer to play.

He stood there behind his ball for a long moment, looking at the green. He was just about to ask for his six-iron when Joanie handed him the six-iron.

The crowd was now totally uncontrollable, and approximately 100,000 spectators were packed around the $18^{th}$ hole and clubhouse area. The noise was amplified and deafening.

The restraining ropes went down, a flood of people spilled onto the fairway, and the crowd control staff were ineffective. The entire $18^{th}$ hole was covered with people.

The crowd pushed themselves back enough for Hummer to make his next swing. He took 5 practice swings and stepped in. In a moment's time, 100,000 avid fans all held their breath in anticipation.

The stroke was pure, it flew high towards the pin, hit the green rolled up, and stopped 10 inches from the hole.

The massive throng of spectators went crazy, the radio and television commentators also went nuts. The world of golf and its long history was about to change forever. It was going to be a miracle for sure.

It took quite some time before the hole could be completed. Just getting through the crammed people was a monumental task. Finally, the other players putted and got out of the way.

Hummer put his ball down, picked up his marker, took little time, and tapped it in.

It became an instant mob scene. Euphoria set in. Hummer picked up his ball and started to throw it to the crowd when a PGA official stopped him. "This ball is destined for the PGA Tour museum, Mr. Muller. As well as your clubs. Congratulations, you just scored a '54'."

They couldn't move; it was like being a sardine in a can. There was no room to maneuver. Hummer and Joanie just looked at each other and beamed.

The main scoreboard now read, "54 – HE DID IT!" The gigantic celebration mimicked the end of a world war.

Neither Hummer nor Joanie could figure out what might happen next. They tried to think. They knew they had to move off the green, as other players still needed to finish their rounds. But there were so many people that it wouldn't be easy to move in any direction. Somehow, their sister Susan made it through, with their mother and father in tow. They all hugged each other. Never would they have dreamed of witnessing such a huge, spectacular, and unbelievable event.

Finally, the mammoth crowd gave way. Hummer made his way to the scorer's tent, where two PGA officials escorted him inside to validate his scorecard. One of the officials claimed the original scorecard for historical reasons.

## VISION 54
### by Dudley Peters

When Hummer came out, the press swarmed him; there must have been twenty microphones thrust toward his face. TV cameras were everywhere, and patrons were taking selfies and seeking autographs. It was a glut. Interviews were conducted with Joanie, the other two golfers, and even his family. All this excitement was happening even as play continued on the course.

When all the players had completed round one, the leaderboard showed Hummer with a 13-stroke lead after the first day of the four-day tournament. The golfing world was stunned. The announcers, writers, old pros, and the biggest names in the sport were at a loss for words. Still, they were all congratulatory and happy for Hummer. Meanwhile, the tournament organizers were adjusting tee times for the next day. They wanted Hummer in the final group—a no-brainer. This decision would benefit advertisers, TV and radio coverage, and, most importantly, crowd control.

Annika Sörenstam arranged with a PGA Tour official to speak privately with Hummer. They met in one of the tents. Annika extended her hand, and Hummer shook it.

"I knew this would happen one day," she said to him.

Hummer replied, "I was sixteen when I picked up an old golf magazine and read about you predicting this in an interview, at least ten years ago."

"Well, you did it, and I watched you do it. It was truly great. I'm happy I was here in person."

# VISION 54
## by Dudley Peters

"Thank you, thank you very much," he said.

She shook his hand again, then left. Hummer returned to be with Joanie and his family. They didn't know it at the time, but this was going to be a long day.

The crowd of reporters, golf correspondents, golf lovers, and others surrounded Hummer. He surprised himself and Joanie with his calmness and how well he handled the unique circumstances. One journalist, Jim Parker, handed Hummer his card and said, "Please contact me for a private interview where we can discuss payment for an exclusive on the 54 you carded today. The earlier, the better. I'd like to hear from you tonight or early in the morning."

Hummer handed the card to Joanie. Almost three hours had passed since he made that final putt. A look from Joanie let Hummer know she wanted to go. A few minutes later, they left. When they got to their rooms, they immediately turned on the TV. The golf story was everywhere. After watching it on several different channels, Hummer finally got into the shower.

Joanie came to his room. All nine of them decided to eat together. They went to the Texas Steak House across the street from the hotel. All nine of them were seated at the same table.

They had a great time at dinner. The steaks were wonderful, and so was the conversation. Near the end of dinner, Brad got everyone's attention. "Joanie informed me about an offer made to Hummer that needs a quick response. I think we should go back to the hotel for a meeting pronto. Everyone here is welcome."

"Let's go," said Hummer. Brad, Tommy, Tim, Adam, Joanie, and Hummer were the only ones in attendance; the parents and sister decided to skip.

Brad wanted to discuss the exclusive interview offer before calling Mr. Parker. He said, "One of us needs to be Hummer's agent for this call. Any takers?"

Adam said, "I think it should be either you or Tommy."

Tim agreed. Brad asked, "What do you think, Joanie?"

"I agree with Adam and Tim."

"Me too," said Hummer.

Brad said, "How about it, Tommy? Why don't you be his agent, at least for today?"

"I'd be happy to if you agree," Tommy replied.

"Okay, you got the job."

Tommy put his phone on speaker and then dialed the number. Mr. Parker answered before the second ring. Tommy introduced himself as Hummer's agent. Mr. Parker asked if Hummer was there.

Hummer said, "I'm here, Mr. Parker!" After exchanging pleasantries, they got down to business. The accepted offer for the exclusive interview was $100,000. Everyone was elated. The interview would be early Monday morning in Augusta, Georgia, at a TV studio there. Tommy agreed.

# **Chapter 29**

Day 2 of the tournament began early Friday; it was cut day, and the field would be reduced to 70 players at the end of the day's play. The 100,000 ticket holders wouldn't all be present until around noon. However, about 50,000 patrons were already on-site.

The media coverage was staggering. Hummer was all over the news, as every station reported on his eighteen-birdie round of golf. They couldn't get enough.

Hummer and his team planned to arrive around 10:30 AM. They left the hotel and pulled into the players' parking area at 10:15 AM. Hummer's tee time was 2:05 PM at hole #1.

During the time before his tee-off, he was mobbed by the media and patrons, all wanting something—photos, autographs, interviews, and more. The patron count was getting very large once again.

His tee time finally arrived, and he was hitting first. He felt so good; he couldn't believe he was about to earn $100,000 from a TV interview. If he were to win the tournament, the winner's share would be over 1 million dollars.

Crowd control was much improved. There was a second line of restraining ropes and an announced threat of ejection for any ticket holder who did not comply. The crowd was around 90,000 strong.

Hummer was once more introduced to the crowd, receiving a huge roar of applause. He stepped up, hit a nice long drive onto the first cut, then hit a soft 9-iron onto the green to about 13 feet. He made the putt for yet another birdie. The crowd roared again.

On the next hole, however, some of his golfing concentration slipped. He got into trouble off the tee, then missed his putt for par, making a bogey. The birdie run was over.

He then made three pars in a row but bogeyed hole #6. His concentration on playing his best golf had gone missing. He had come back down to earth.

Joanie abruptly picked up on it. She grabbed him by the arm on the next hole, put her face right in front of his, and said, "Snap out of it right now, and do not make me say this again."

"What?"

"What! Daydreaming, that's what, and I mean it," she barked.

"Sorry," he said.

Hummer thought he could simply snap right back to playing his best golf, but he soon found out it would require extreme determination and a lot of effort to make this happen. Plus, the forces somehow worked against all golfers perpetually.

Joanie might have caught all this just in time.

At the end of the round, he posted a 70, a mere 2 under par. However, at the end of the day's play, he still held an 11-stroke lead going into Saturday.

Saturday's play still had Hummer in the final group. With only 70 players, the start was a little later. Hummer was going off at 2:05 PM.

The media coverage did virtually no reporting on the 70 Hummer carded yesterday. Ninety-nine point nine percent of the coverage was about his 54 on Thursday. They played the same footage over and over again.

At 2:05 PM, Hummer was introduced again to the mass of spectators. As he stepped up, got ready, and connected, something felt wrong. His desire was fading, and his mind was wandering. It was like a different person was playing. His score on the front nine was 37, a disappointing one over par. The announcers barely made any negative comments, though; after all, he was their new sensation.

Then, they made the turn, and Hummer came to life. He birdied 10, 11, and 12 for three in a row. He made pars on 13, 14, and 15, then eagled 16. Once again, the announcers got all excited and hyped up. He made par on 17 and birdied 18, finishing with a score of 30 on the back nine for a total score of 67. He now had a lead of 13 strokes going into the final round.

The mass of patrons, as well as the media, were extremely happy with what they saw. Once again, golf was on nearly every program, with different commentators reporting on the Texas Open.

Sunday morning arrived. Joanie knocked on Hummer's door. She took a seat in a chair and looked at Hummer, who was still in bed.

Hummer asked, "What is it?"

Joanie did not answer right away. After a long pause, she said, "I'm having difficulty grasping what has happened to you, me, and our family. I couldn't sleep last night. Tomorrow we will be rich, far beyond any dream we might have had. Plus, what you have done will bring us even more wealth, endorsements, and so much more. How will we handle this? I'm worried."

"I believe you're right. I have an idea. We could turn over control of the money to Susan. She is, or will be, a CPA, right? Let her handle it. That way, we can relieve ourselves of thinking about it. What do you think?"

"Perfect. That's a wonderful idea. You'd better start getting ready for today."

"Right."

All nine of them had breakfast together. They mainly talked about Hummer being on TV everywhere. Tommy said, "We'd better start focusing on today and what's going to happen. When Hummer finishes the round, we need to be aware of safety. I'm sure he will be mobbed, so keep that in mind."

They arrived at 10:15 again today. His tee time was 1:15 PM, just like before.

The masses were there early; by 9 AM, almost all ticket holders had arrived. Just about all eyes were on Hummer. During his introduction at the first tee, the roar and applause were so loud that Hummer was told to wait before hitting his drive. It was three minutes before he was given the green light. There was a roar after every shot he hit all day, even the bad ones. At the end of the round, Hummer scored a 69. He won the tournament by 12 strokes. His total of 260 set a new record for the Texas Open.

The winner's share of the purse was $1.6 million. As expected, offers started coming in from golf equipment companies, ball companies, golf clothing companies, and for endorsements. He was going to need a professional manager for sure. Everything was happening at supersonic speed, and it needed to be handled properly.

They got into Augusta late Sunday night. Augusta National had arranged a six-bedroom house for Hummer to use during the Masters Tournament. Brad, Tommy, Tim, and Adam managed to get rooms at a nearby motel. Tommy made arrangements to pick up Hummer and Joanie in the morning to take them to the TV studio.

# Chapter 30

## The Interview

Jim Parker met them in the lobby and led them to the green room. The staff primped Hummer and made sure he was photogenic for TV. Mr. Parker briefed Hummer on what to expect. He let him know that it was going to be a taped interview that could be edited if necessary.

Surprisingly, Hummer was not at all nervous. He was calm and ready. Moments later, he was led to the set. There were two high-back chairs there. The background was a mural of Augusta National.

A stage manager announced, "The take starts in 5 seconds, 4, 3, 2, 1, action."

Jim Parker made an opening statement regarding the reasons for the interview; this took about two minutes. Then he turned to Hummer. The opening question was:

"Tell us, Hummer, how did you do it?"

"Well, I'll answer that question this way: practice, practice, practice, and then more practice. It takes a very long time to hit a million golf shots. I've done that. I love golf so much I never get tired of playing or practicing. I believe that there is such a thing as luck, too. Plus, I think you can make your own luck at certain times and under certain conditions."

"Is it true that you haven't had any lessons from a golf instructor?"

"Yes, that is correct. The pro at Briar Lakes says that I am a natural."

"Let me ask you this: did you ever dream that you would do this?"

"Yes, I sure did. I was 16 at the time. I picked up an old golf magazine and read about Annika Sorenstam, predicting that it would happen one day. I had a short dream that I would be the one to do it. But I should add, I forgot all about it three seconds later."

"After being an unknown to becoming the only golfer in the world to score 18 birdies in one round of golf, a round that was seen live by millions of people all around the world, what do you have to say?"

"I don't know how to answer that one. I guess I'm just happy that golf fans got to see it happen live."

"Is there anything else you would like to add?"

"Yes, family. My family—I owe everything to my family. They brought me up the right way, the proper way, the honest way. My younger sister saved me more than once from personal disaster when I was a teenager. Whatever I may achieve from golf will go to my family, that's for sure."

"What a wonderful thing to say, Hummer. Thank you for your candor."

"May I say something?"

"Sure."

"I would like to say that the members of the PGA Tour that I have met so far are, without a doubt, the nicest, most respectable, and most honest people anyone could ever want to be associated with. They all have my highest admiration."

"Hummer, let me close with this: how do you think you will do in the Masters this week?"

"I don't know; I've never played here. But on the other hand, I had never played The Oaks Course either. I will say this, with Joanie at my side, she will see to it that

I'll give it my very best."

# READERS BONUS

Here are some betting games listed that you and your golfing buddies might enjoy. I personally think that modest gaming on private matches increases the enjoyment of golf, win or lose. (The author)

Gaming    (another word for gambling)

Exposure   (amount of money you can lose on a particular bet.)

Mutations  (modifications of Golf Formats and Wagers)

(The next pages will have information about different ways to gamble on golf.)

In this section, there's a list of dozens of different tournament formats and side games. Each of these games has its own rules and we go a little more in-depth in the explanation. So check below on the name of the format, or bet to read about it:

3-2 Bet

3 in 1 Bet

3 little pigs or (3 blind mice) Bet

40 Balls

6-Point Game

Acey Ducey

Air Press Bet

Appearances bet

Arnie bet

## VISION 54
### by Dudley Peters

Auto win

Bag raid bet

Barkies bet

Bear bet

Best at something bet, or "the rack"

Best to worst, or "on the spot" bet

Bingo Bango Bongo

Bridge, or "name that score" bet (not for beginners)

Chippies bet

COD bet  or round-robin

Clink, or Klink

Criers and Whiners

Defender

Eliminator

Fairways and greens, or F&G

Favorite holes

Fish

Five clubs

Fort Lauderdale

Greenies

Gruesome

Hog  or Wolf

Honest John

Jack and Jill

Las Vegas

Long and short

Longest yard

Low Putts

Modified Pinehurst

Modified Stableford

Money Ball

Mulligans

Murphy

Mutt & Jeff

Nassau

No putts

N.O.S.E. game

Oozles & Foozles

Pinnie or Polee

Scruffy

Shazam

Skirts

Snakes

Stealies

Strike three

Switch

T & F Game

Three blind mice:

Train Wreck

Triples

WAD

Wolfman, or Wolf

Yellow Ball or Lone Ranger

Plus, there are Many, Many More Formats, Games, and Bets ... these above are just some of the most popular.

You can read how to use the games; you can run down the basics of many more formats. So, go through them, find a game you like (and read the explanation).

Here we go!

3-2: (or Three-Two) or Thirty-Two

A side game that is essentially a challenge from one golfer to another to avoid a three-putt. The golfer who issues the challenge is giving 3-to-2 odds that the challenged golfer can't get his ball into the hole in fewer than three putts.

The challenged golfer usually has the option to decline the bet, but some groups play it as automatic when the challenge is issued. If the golfer who issues the challenge wins the bet (meaning the challenged golfer 3-putts or worse), he wins two units of the bet. If the challenged golfer gets it in the hole in two putts or fewer, he wins three units of the bet.

3 in 1 (Three in One)

VISION 54
by Dudley Peters

A format for a group of four golfers playing 2-vs.-2, 3 in 1 refers to the fact that three different formats are played over the 18 holes of the bet. The format changes every six holes, for example:

Holes 1-6, better ball

Holes 7-12, alternate shot

Holes 13-18, 2-man scramble

Make the formats anything you want. Three-in-one is typically played as a single, 18-hole bet, but you can split it up into three different 6-hole bets (each new format is a new bet) if you prefer.

3 Little Pigs: - See below (under Three Blind Mice) a 4-Point Game
Format for a group of four golfers, playing two per side. Each golfer plays his or her own ball throughout. On each hole, four points are at stake:

Two points for the lower of each side's low scores, one point for the lower of each side's high scores, and one point for the low team total.

Ties award no points, and winning the low individual score with a birdie results in double points (4 instead of 2).

'Acey Ducey': or 'Aces and Deuces'

Acey Ducey, also called Aces and Deuces, is a betting game best for groups of four golfers. On each hole, the low score (the "ace") wins an agreed-upon amount from the other three players, and the high score (the "deuce") loses an agreed-upon amount to the other three players. Our Most Popular Betting Games top-10 list includes an example using dollar amounts, so check that out for more.

Air Press:

An "air press" is a bet that Golfer A calls against Golfer B when Golfer B's drive is still in the air, and Golfer A has not yet played his or her own drive.

When Golfer A calls an air press in such circumstances, A is betting that he will post a better score on the hole than B. Groups that play air presses typically make them automatic (when one is called, it can't be declined). Re-presses are allowed, however, so when A hits his or her own drive, B can re-repress while A's ball is still airborne, doubling the bet.

Appearances:

A side bet more commonly called Honors. After the order of play is determined randomly on the first tee, the golfer who wins the honor of playing first on each successive tee wins the Appearances bet. The bet can have a monetary value or point value.

Arnie:

Named after Arnold Palmer, it's a side bet that goes to any golfer who makes par on a hole without ever being in the fairway. Wins a predetermined amount from each other golfers.

Auto Win:

VISION 54
by Dudley Peters

Played by any group (two, three or four golfers), an Auto Win bet is automatically won (hence the name) by any golfer doing one of these three things on a hole:

Chip-in from off the green (fringes don't count);

Hole-out from a sand bunker;

Stick an approach shot inside the flagstick from 150 yards out or more or on any par-3 hole.

Most groups award only one "Auto Win" per hole, so if more than one of these things happens, the golfer accomplishing one first on the hole gets it.

Barkies: (or Woodies)

The bark (or wood) in question belongs to trees. A "barkie" ("woody") is a bet that is won by a golfer who makes par on a hole after hitting a tree. A "double barkie" doubles the bet and is achieved by making par after hitting two trees on a hole. Hitting leaves doesn't count; your ball must contact solid wood.

The Bear:

Betting game for groups of golfers (three or four works best) where the object is to win a hole (with the low score of the group) and to hold that position after the 9th and 18th holes. The first golfer who wins a hole "captures the bear" and holds it until a different golfer captures it. Each time the bear changes owners, the original bet doubles. The golfer who holds the bear after No. 9 wins the pot for the front 9. The bear is then set free, and the game starts over on No. 10. The holder of the bear on No. 18 wins the next pot.

Best the Worst: (or "On the Spot")

A game for groups of three or four golfers. Golfers rotate being "on the spot," one golfer per hole. That golfer's job is to beat the worst score among the other golfers in the group on that hole. If Golfer A is on the spot and makes 5, while the other golfers in the group score 4, 4 and 6, Golfer A wins the bet.

'Bag Raid' or 'Pick Up Sticks'

The game that goes by the names Bag Raid or Pick Up Sticks is a match play game between two golfers. Player A and Player B tee off and play match play. And each time one wins a hole, his opponent gets to remove a club from the winner's bag: Every time you win a hole, your opponent raids your bag and selects a club to remove from play.

Every time you lose a hole, you reach into your opponent's bag and take one of his clubs out of play.

To reiterate: The loser of a hole gets to remove a club from the winner's bag. In theory, that helps level the playing field over the course of the round. Bag Raid can be played with all clubs vulnerable to removal, or you and your opponent can agree before teeing off to exempt the putter.

Best At Something, or "The Rack":

VISION 54
by Dudley Peters

This is a points-based betting game that can be played alongside any other type of match in which golfers are playing their own balls throughout. Points are awarded or subtracted for different things throughout the round, most commonly in this fashion:

Fairway hit, +1 point

Green in regulation, +1

1-putt green, +1

3 putts or more on a green, -1 point

Hitting into a hazard, -1

Lost ball, -1

Out of bounds, -1

Tally points at the end and high points wins the agreed-upon bet.

Bingle Bangle Bongle:

Bingle- first player to hit fairway, Bangle- first player to hit green, Bongle – first player to hole out.  Also called Bingo, Bango, and Bongo  (very popular beginners bet.) played on every hole.

Bridge: (or 'Name That Score')

In Bridge, a set amount of points or money applies to each hole. This amount is agreed upon before the round. When stepping up to a tee box, one team makes a "bid" on the number of strokes (net or gross - decide beforehand, obviously) they think it will take them to play the hole. (The format is usually played 2-vs.-2, but 1-vs.-1 also works.)

Say you're at a tough par-4. You and your partner bid 11. You are offering a bet (of the set amount) to the other team that your side can play the hole in no more than 11 strokes.

The other side has three options:

Take the bet;

Or take the bet and double it, or bid lower than 11.

If the other side is confident it can beat 11 strokes, it will bid 10. Then it's back to your team: Take the bet, take the bet and double it, or bid 9 strokes. If one team takes the bet and doubles it, then the other team has the option of doubling back (meaning that if you're playing for money, carefully consider how much you're playing for because it can add up quickly). Which team opens the bidding on the first hole is determined randomly. On each ensuing hole, the team that lost the previous hole opens the bidding.

Chippies:

Chip in from off the green, and you win the chippie - either the monetary value of the bet or the point value if (as is often the case) chippies are being played as part of Dots/Garbage-type games.

C.O.D.

## VISION 54
### by Dudley Peters

Another name for a Round Robin (a k a Sixes or Hollywood) format. The initials "C.O.D." derive from this formulation for rotating partners:

C (Cart): On holes 1-6, you partner with the golfer with whom you are sharing the cart.

O (Opposites):

On holes 7-12, the driver of one cart partners the passenger in the other, and vice-versa.

D (Drivers): On holes 13-18, the drivers of the two carts partner with one another, as do the passengers in each cart.

Clink or Klink - A popular game, 2 vs 2 or 1 vs. 1. This is a 7-way game. (1. Front nine, 2. Front nine out only press, 3. Back nine. 4. Back nine out only press, 5, the 18-hole bet is double. 6. Then the 18-hole outpress only goes back to the original amount. All bets are automatic. (maximum win/loss, 7 ways.) All bets are equal except for the overall 18 bets, Whose value is double.

A $2 clink is played. The maximum you can win is $14, and the maximum you can lose is $14.

Criers and Whiners: (also called Replay, No Alibis, Play It Again Sam or Wipe Out)

This game of many names takes a golfer's handicap and converts them into do-overs or mulligans. Have a course handicap of 14? You get 14 mulligans to use during the round. The game can be played with full handicaps, as just cited, but it is most common to use only three-fourths or two-thirds of handicaps. That forces the player to be judicious in using his replay strokes. Two other conditions usually apply: The first tee shot of the day may not be replayed, and no shot can be replayed twice.

Eliminator:

Tournament format for 4-person teams or a betting game for several groups of four. Also known as In the Bucket, it is a best-ball format with a twist: As a player's score is used for the team score, he is "eliminated" from counting as the team score on ensuing holes until only one player is left whose score is eligible to be used (then the process starts over).

Example:

Players A, B, C and D tee off on Hole 1. Player A is the low-ball on the first hole. All players move on to Hole 2, but Player A's score can't be used; Players B, C, and D are eligible. On the second hole, Player B is the low-ball. All players move on to Hole 3, but the scores of A and B are now ineligible; only C and D have a chance to provide the team score.

On No. 3, Player C is a low score. And that leaves Player D as the lone survivor - his score must be used on the fourth hole as the team score. On Hole 5, the rotation starts over.

Fairways & Greens: (or F&G's)

## VISION 54
### by Dudley Peters

This is a betting game best for groups of golfers with similar handicaps. The object is, of course, to hit fairways and greens. The catch is that you have to be the only player in your group to hit the fairway (off the tee) to win the bet or the only player in your group to hit the green (in regulation) to win the bet.

Determine before the round the value of each fairway and each green. Each hole (excluding par-3s) has two bets - one for the fairway and one for the green. If two or more players find the fairway or two or more players are on the green in regulation, then that bet carries over to the following hole (ala skins).

Fairway & Greens can also be played for points. Each golfer in a group tracks his points earned through the round. At the end of the round, high points wins an overall bet (the amount of which is set before the round).

Favorite Holes:

Before the round, each golfer in your group ponies up the agreed-upon amount of money for the Favorite Holes pot. Next, each golfer circles three holes on his scorecard - his favorite holes, the ones where he typically scores great. At the end of the round, each golfer tallies up his total on those three favorite holes, and a low score wins the pot.

Fish:

A side game for a group of golfers that includes bets on three separate achievements relating to birdies:

The golfer who makes the first birdie in the round wins one bet;

The golfer who makes the longest birdie putt during the round wins a bet;

And the golfer who makes the most birdies during the round wins a third bet.   Just remember first-longest-most.

Five of Clubs:

A tournament format in which each golfer has to choose only five of his clubs to use during the tournament. Variations in the format revolve around how the putter is treated. Sometimes, the putter doesn't count as

one of your five clubs; however, in most cases, when Five of Clubs is played, the putter does count as one of your five.

Fort Lauderdale:

While there may be some regional variations in the specifics, when a tournament is using the Fort Lauderdale name it is usually just a typical scramble format. In other words, Fort Lauderdale is usually just a synonym for a scramble.

Greenies:

A "greenie" is a side bet that automatically pays off for any golfer who records a green in regulation. Greenies are commonly included in the game known as Garbage, Trash, or Dots. A group using greenies only has to agree before the round starts that a) greenies are in effect and b) how much - in monetary value or in points - each greenie is worth. The group then tees off, and every time during the round a greenie is recorded by a golfer, the golfer marks it down. At the end of the round, golfers compare how many greenies each recorded, tally up the points or money, and pay out the differences.

Gruesomes:

Gruesomes is a 2-person team game that is more common as a betting game but is also sometimes used as a golf tournament format.

In Gruesomes, both members of Team A hit drives. Then, the members of the opposing side (Team B) select which drive Team A has to play. When Team B's golfers tee off, Team A selects which drive *they* have to play. Needless to say, when you're choosing which of two drives your opponents have to play, you're going to make them play the worse - or most gruesome - of the two drives.

Following the selection of the tee balls, the teams play out the hole in alternate shot fashion, except that the player who hit the "gruesome" tee ball also plays the second shot for his side.

Hog or wolf:

Hog is very similar to Defender and Wolf. On each hole, one player in a group of four golfers is designated as the Hog, and the order rotates through the round (A on No. 1, B on No. 2, C on No. 3, D on No. 4, then back to A and so on).

by Dudley Peters

In Hog, all members of the group tee off, then the "Hog" has two options: "hog" the hole by playing against the other three players, or pick one of the other three players as a partner for the hole, making it 2-on-2. The one lowball wins the hole.

If the "Hog" plays 1-vs.-3 and wins the hole, he gets 3 points;

If he loses the hole, the other three golfers get 1 point each.

If the "Hog" chooses a partner and wins, both players get 1 point; if they lose, the other two players get 1 point each.

Honest John:

Before the round starts, members of your group each put an agreed-upon dollar amount into the pot. Each player predicts the score they will shoot for the round and writes it down. At the end of the round, they compare their actual score to their predicted score. Who came closest to shooting his or her predicted score? The golfer who did wins the Honest John pot.

Jack and Jill:

When a tournament is called a "Jack and Jill," it means that it is a team event in which men and women are paired together to form the teams.

Las Vegas:

A betting game: A 2-vs.-2 contest in which the partners' scores are paired to form one number. In Las Vegas, they are paired with the low number going first. Player A makes 5; Player B makes 6, that combines to form 56.

In Daytona, which number goes first depends on whether either player made par or better. If one of the partners makes par or better, you combine the scores to form the lowest number. But if both golfers on a side make a bogey or worse, their scores are combined to form the highest number. If on a par-4, the partners make a 5 and 7, that becomes not 57 but 75. This game is not for beginners.

Long and Short:

A format for 2-person teams. The name explains the game: One member of the team plays the long shots (drives and approaches), while the other member of the team plays the short shots (pitches, chips, and putts). In order to avoid potential disagreements between teams over which player should play certain shots, it's advisable for the Long and Short Tournament organizers to set specific yardage that delineates the "long" and "short."

Longest Yard:

Betting game for groups of two, three or four golfers in which the yardage of a hole determines how many points that hole is worth. If you have a low score on a hole that is, for example, 380 yards long, then you win 380 points. Win a 125-yard hole, and you get 125 points. No points are awarded on holes without an outright winner. Set the point value carefully because there might be 7,000 points total at stake, depending on yardages.

Low Putts:

In a Low Putts tournament, you throw out all your other strokes and only count putts. And the golfer or team with the fewest putts is the Low Putts winner. Before the round, agree on the value of the bet (each member of your group puts in an equal amount), and after the round, count putts. The golfer with the Low Putts wins the pot.

Murphy:

A Murphy bet usually happens on the final hole of a match. The player, or 2-man team, that is behind or losing his bets calls for a Murphy; it means that he, or they, will play this one hole for every bet (double or nothing.)

Mutt and Jeff:

Tournament format or a side bet in which the focus is on par-3 holes and par-5 holes only. The round of golf is completed, and then the total net score for each player or each group on the par-3 and par-5 holes is recorded. The low net on those long and short holes is the winner.

NASSAU:

(Front nine + back nine + overall 18) 3-way bet; sometimes the overall 18 is worth double. Probably the most common golf game used for gambling, especially when presses are used. (best way to be introduced into betting on your ability to play golf.)

No Putts: (or Everything but Putts)

## VISION 54
### by Dudley Peters

Are you a great tee-to-green but a lousy putter? Talk your opponents into a No Putts bet. Keep track of putts throughout the round. At the end of the round, throw out all the putts. How many strokes are left? That's your No Putts score.

N.O.S.E. Tournament:

Golfers count their scores only on holes that begin with the letters - N, O, S, E. That means holes one, six, seven, eight, nine, eleven, sixteen, seventeen and eighteen. (You play the full course, but only count scores on those holes for your NOSE score.) As a tiebreaker, low putts, on the N.O.S.E. holes only, are commonly used.

Oozles and Foozles:

Oozles are good, Foozles are bad, in this bet played on par-3 holes.

Version 1: Closest to the pin on a par-3 wins the Oozle (worth one betting unit), provided he holes out in two or fewer putts.

He would get the Foozle, the loss of one betting unit if he 3-putts.

Version 2: Closest to the pine on the par-3 automatically wins the Oozle - unless he then 3-putts or worse, then he would get the Foozle.

Want more action? Extend Oozles and Foozles to all holes, not just par-3s.

Pinnie or a Polee:

A side bet that is automatically won by achieving one thing.

(first case) stopping any approach shot inside the length of the flagstick.

In the second case, a distance requirement is usually applied (say, the approach shot must be 100+ yards or 150+ yards).

There is another option: the pinnie or polee might be available only to the first golfer to stop an approach shot from 150+ yards within the length of the flagstick.

Scruffy:

When "scruffies" are played, a golfer in a group can invoke a scruffy bet after any one of his drives, good, bad or otherwise. However, scruffies are not automatic, and the other members of the group can decline to accept the bet. If the bet is accepted, the golfer who issued the scruffy is betting he'll make par on the hole. Therefore, scruffies are traditionally issued (and especially accepted) following poor drives.

Shazam:

A betting game played on the green, in which golfers bet on the chance that another golfer will 3-putt. Once a golfer has reached the green and at any time before he putts, one or more of the other players in the group may call out "Shazam." When another golfer calls out "Shazam," the one putting is forced into a bet with that player. If all three other members of a four-ball Shazam are the putter, then the putter has a bet with each of them.

The outcome of the bet varies depending on how many putts the Shazammed golfer then takes:

A 3-putt results in the golfer who was Shazammed, losing the bet.

If he 4-putts, he loses double the bet.

If he 1-putts, he wins double the bet.

If he 2-putts, no money changes hands.

A player may also Shazam himself if he is outside one flagstick-length from the hole, thereby forcing a bet with all other members of the group. A golfer who Shazams himself wins the bet by 1-putting but loses double if he 3-putts.

Skirts:

You know how some charitable golf tournaments sell mulligans before the tourney tees off? "Skirts" describes a similar situation, but in the case of "skirts," what is for sale is the ability for the golfer who buys a skirt to tee off from the forward tees (a k a, the ladies' tees). Let's say tournament organizers are offering "skirts" for $5 each. You buy three of them. You now have the right, during the tournament round, to tee off from the forward tees three times during the round.

Snakes:

2-3-4 players. A 3-putt gets a snake, the next 3-putt gets a snake, plus all the other snakes from the player that had them, etc. Before play begins, the price is agreed upon. The important part of this bet is that the "away" ball, on the green, must hit the next putt.

Stealies:

Used in conjunction with a closest-to-the-pin contest or bet. When Stealies are in effect, the losers of the closest-to-the-pin get a chance to steal away the prize or wager. Say a group has agreed to a CP bet on each of the par-3s during the round. Golfer A, B, C, and D hit their tee shots on the first par-3, and Golfer C is closest to the pin. So Golfer C wins the bet. But A, B, and D can steal away the bet if one of them then birdies the hole (and C does not). The birdie can be holed from anywhere on the course (chip-in, etc.). (The CKP winner can still keep the bet, however, by making his own birdie.)

Strike Three:

At the end of your round of golf, look over your scorecard. Find your three highest individual hole scores ... and erase them. Add up your score without those three holes, and that's your Strike Three score. Low score wins.

Sundowner:

A term for any golf tournament that is played in the late afternoon but mostly applied to 9-hole tournaments. Especially when those events are part of a golf league's weekly schedule.

Sometimes, the term "sundowner" is applied to such leagues themselves, as in a "sundowner league."

Switch:

Can be a tournament format or a betting game for a group of four playing 2-vs.-2. Either way, it involves 2-person teams on which the players Switch balls following the tee shots, then play out the hole using those balls. After the drives, Player A walks to Player B's ball and plays it from there into the hole. And Player B takes over A's tee ball. Use the combined score of both golfers or the one low ball of the side.

T and F: (or T&F)

In a T and F tournament, holes whose numbers begin with "t" or "f" - Nos. 3 and 4, for example - holes hold special significance. There are two ways the format is played most commonly:

With teams of three or more, or in individual competition, a T and F tournament counts only scores recorded on holes beginning with "t" or "f." There are nine of those holes, four on the front nine, five on the back nine (holes 2, 3, 4, 5, 10, 12, 13, 14, 15).

With 2-person teams, one person's scores are used on the "t" and "f" holes, and the other partner's scores are used on the remaining nine holes.

Threesome:

A Threesome match is one in which one golfer competes against a team of two golfers, the team of two playing alternate shots.

The Train Wreck:

In The Train Wreck, points are awarded to a golfer who makes par or better:

Par - 1 point

Birdie - 2 points

Eagle - 5 points

Obviously, you want to finish the round with the most points to win the tournament or the bet. But, if at any point in the round, you make two bogeys in a row - or one double-bogey - you lose all your points and start over again at zero.

Three Blind Mice: (or Three Little Pigs)

Version 1:

A tournament format. After the round, tournament organizers randomly draw three numbers from 1 through 18. Those three holes are thrown out. Golfers add up their scores on the remaining holes, and those are the scores for the round.

Version 2:

More often, a bet, at the end of the round, each golfer throws out his three worst scores of the round. Add up the 15 remaining holes. That's your score.

Triples:

A format or bet for groups of three golfers. A point value is assigned to a player's standing on each hole:

6 points for having the best score on a hole;

4 points for the middle score;

2 points for the worst score.

For ties, the points are added together and divided by the number of players tied. Two examples. For example, if all three golfers tie for a low score - 6 points plus 4 points plus 2 points divided by three equals four points for each. If two players tie for a low score, 6 plus 4 equals 10; 10 divided by 2 equals five points each. The bet can be based on the overall result; i.e., the player with the most points wins the bet of a predetermined amount. Or it can be based on the differential in points between players, with each point worth a set amount.

WAD   (see below)

Wolfman – Wolf:

Similar to Wolf, but Wolfman is a betting game specifically for groups of three players and the "it" player, so to speak, is automatically chosen based on tee shots. On each hole, one of the golfers will be the Wolfman, while the other two are called Hunters.

Here's how the Wolfman is chosen on each hole:

VISION 54
by Dudley Peters

All three players in the group tee off. On par 4s and par 5s, the middle drive (second-longest drive, in other words) becomes the Wolfman;

On par-3 holes, the second closest to the hole is the Wolfman. All three golfers play out the hole at stroke play. The net scores of the two Hunters are added together; the Wolfman's net score is

doubled. If the Wolfman's doubled score is lower than the Hunters' combined score, the Wolfman wins the hole (and the bet). If the Hunters' combined score is lower, they win the hole and bet.

Yellow Ball or Lone Ranger:

This game is mostly used for a one-day event at a tournament or outing. Each 4 man team has one yellow ball. They must take turns being the player using the yellow ball for an entire hole, then pass the yellow ball to the next player for the next hole, etc. The lowest handicap player is first to use it, then the next lowest handicap, etc., and then repeat. The foursome that keeps the yellow the longest without losing it wins a predetermined prize.

WAD BET

(My suggestion) If you are offered a golf bet, that has the word. "WAD" anywhere in its name, run for your car and lock up your wallet in the trunk. Never make a golf bet with someone that employs the word WAD.

VISION 54
by Dudley Peters

Modest gambling on golf can be very exciting and alluring. Also, it can be addictive, but when done properly. It makes the game enjoyment more spicy, so to speak. But never, never, never risk your rent money on it.

*There are more games here than I wanted to mention, but this list will give you some idea of the many, many ways for you and your fellow golfers to review. I recommend that you select only one or two of the ones you might like and forget the rest. Personally, after playing over 40 years of all types of Nassau's, I like the Clink bet best, with trash added in.  Find the one you like. Enjoy.*

# About the Author

The author was born in Shreveport, Louisiana, and now lives in Saint Michaels, Maryland. A passionate golfer for decades, he currently serves as the president of the TBA Tour. He began writing novels for personal enjoyment in 2020, striving to craft engaging and enjoyable stories without curse words or explicit content, ensuring a wholesome reading experience. In an era where some authors might turn to AI for creative assistance, he chooses to rely solely on his own imagination and skill, creating original and authentic works.

In 1940, the author and his family relocated from Shreveport to Maryland. He graduated as Class President from Oxon Hill High School in 1953 and served in the US Navy Reserves from 1953 to 1961. He married his high school sweetheart in 1954, and together they have four children, five grandchildren, and two great-grandchildren. A dedicated entrepreneur, he established a construction business in 1955 and successfully ran it for twenty-five years. During this time, he also contributed to his community through roles such as Master of the Anacostia Masonic Lodge, President of the South Gate Lions Club, and President of the Maryland VIP Club.

His debut novel, Anxiety, launched his writing career. He was followed by The Texan in June 2021 and Fabulous Jane in February

2022. His latest book is his most ambitious to date—a thrilling golf story that he considers the greatest ever written in the genre.